play like
T-Bone Walker

Audio Access Included!

The Ultimate Guitar Lesson
by Dave Rubin

Cover Photo © Getty Images / Val Wilmer

PLAYBACK+
Speed • Pitch • Balance • Loop

To access audio visit:
www.halleonard.com/mylibrary

Enter Code
4314-0768-9768-5844

ISBN: 978-1-5400-1477-1

Visit Hal Leonard Online at
www.halleonard.com

Contact Us:
Hal Leonard
7777 West Bluemound Road
Milwaukee, WI 53213
Email: info@halleonard.com

In Europe, contact:
Hal Leonard Europe Limited
42 Wigmore Street
Marylebone, London, W1U 2RN
Email: info@halleonardeurope.com

In Australia, contact:
Hal Leonard Australia Pty. Ltd.
4 Lentara Court
Cheltenham, Victoria, 3192 Australia
Email: info@halleonard.com.au

CONTENTS

INTRODUCTION

"I think if it wasn't for the blues, there wouldn't be no jazz."
–T-Bone Walker

There is much truth to the conventional wisdom that Aaron Thibeaux "T-Bone" Walker is to electric blues guitar what his buddy Charlie Christian is to electric jazz guitar. Not coincidentally, both studied with teacher Chuck Richardson in Oklahoma City. While Christian played jazz with blues roots, Walker played blues with a penchant for jazz melodies and chords. He was (and remains) the cornerstone of post-war electric blues guitar.

Walker was not the first to play or record electric guitar. However, his official debut in 1942 with "Mean Old World" b/w "I Got a Break Baby" was so groundbreaking, it makes literal chronology a moot point. Guitarists were quick to recognize tonalities and sonorities heretofore unheard from the 6-string instrument—be they flat top or arch top acoustic, National steel, or electric. His sound was rich and nuanced with a slight edge, featuring the warm, natural sound that can only come from the perfect interaction of strings, vibrating wood, and high-fidelity single coil pickups on an arch top guitar. Expressive phrasing flowed effortlessly from his fingers through his signature tone.

So come take a "Stroll" with "Bone" and learn the secrets of his style in breadth and depth—from his rhythmically and harmonically sophisticated comping, to his incisive, horn-inflected solos. A broad selection of his greatest songs are analyzed in detail and served up in easily accessible bites. Though "T-Bone" was a play on the pronunciation of his middle name (and not his appetite for steak), be prepared to dig in for a juicy musical repast.

Gear

Though he may have had a brief dalliance with a Strat in the 1960s, Walker epitomized the vibrant amplified sound of robust arch top boxes.

Songs

The hippest aspects of five Walker classics from the late 1940s through the 1950s will be "picked over" in detail.

Essential Licks

Know these finely crafted gems and you will be swinging with the style, grace, and power of Joe DiMaggio.

Signature Riffs

With the suave confidence and skill of a swing jazz man, Walker tossed off timeless blues riffs as jumping off points for his lithe solos.

Integral Techniques

Hidden in the tracks of his songs, and known to the Walker cognoscenti, are the foundation lead lines and chord voicings which contribute to their greatness. Check them out here.

Stylistic DNA

Lurking just below the surface of his music are the genomes that connect Walker to the blues and jazz tradition from which he sprang. Knowing them adds markedly to the appreciation and grasp of his music.

Must Hear

Walker had a long, fruitful recording career. Here are the not-to-be-missed collections to be savored and studied.

Must See

Luckily for blues guitarists, there is a sumptuous selection of Walker videos which show the man in all his jutting guitar swagger and glory.

ABOUT THE AUDIO

To access the audio examples that accompany this book, simply go to **www.halleonard.com/mylibrary** and enter the code found on page 1. This will give you instant access to every example. The examples that include audio are marked with an audio icon throughout the book.

GEAR:
THE SOUND OF AN ELECTRIC BLUES PIONEER

Guitars

Most of the earliest photos of T-Bone Walker show him with a Gibson ES-250. Making its debut in 1940, the guitar was essentially a more deluxe version of the Gibson ES-150 (the first commercially successful electric guitar created in 1936). Significant changes to the ES-250 included: large, block-type fingerboard markers, a pickup with individual "blade" pole pieces, and the Super 400 tailpiece. In some photos he is also seen with a Gibson ES-300 with double-parallelogram markers and an ES-250 pickup.

The iconic T-Bone Walker guitar, however, is the Gibson triple P-90 pickup ES-5, which was itself an outgrowth of the "super deluxe" Super 400. A 1949 model (later refretted and sporting newer knobs) is seen in photos more often than any other blues machine. Contributing to its special aural characteristics is the unique sound of the single coil pickups being wired "out of phase," either deliberately (others are reported with the "mod") or by accident. There is also a rare photo showing him performing in London with a borrowed, funky Burns Virginian amplified flat top.

Sometime in the 1960s, when his ES-5 was stolen on an English tour, Walker began playing a Gibson Barney Kessel regular model (1961–74) with double-parallelogram fretboard markers. After the ES-5, it is the guitar seen most often in photos. Though it is reported he also played an ES-335 at some point, no photo was found during research, and the Kessel model appears to be the only humbucking-pickup guitar he ever slung across his shoulder.

Amps

Walker likely first played his ES-250 through a Gibson EH-185 amp, before moving on to Fenders in the 1950s. Photos show Walker playing through a 1952–53 tweed "TV-front" Fender Bassman with a 15" Jensen speaker, a narrow panel 1955–60 tweed Twin, and possibly, a 1961–62 "piggyback" white Tolex Bassman.

Picks

Not known—though genuine tortoise shell (since banned) would be an educated guess.

Effects

He had four: his index, middle, ring, and pinky fingers.

SONGS

Mean Old World (1942)
From *T-Bone Walker: The Ultimate Collection 1929–57* (Acrobat)

Originally recorded by pre-war blues guitarist Bill Gaither as "Mean Old World (to Live in)" in 1938, the Walker classic was not released until 1945. It was part of a set of 10-inch 78 RPM records also including "I Got a Break Baby." In 1947, it was re-released as the "A" side of a single platter, with "I Got a Break Baby" as the "B" side. Its importance to the world of electric blues guitar can hardly be overstated. Saxophone players may have been hearing footsteps…

Intro

Two 12-bar blues choruses preceded by a four-measure chordal Intro is as good an introduction to the guitar artistry of T-Bone Walker as could be wanted. The first four measures of the Intro contain an example of what would become his classic broken 9th chord sequence: the I chord "walking down" to the ♭VII to the ♭VI to the V chord within two measures, and then repeating.

Mean Old World
Example 1

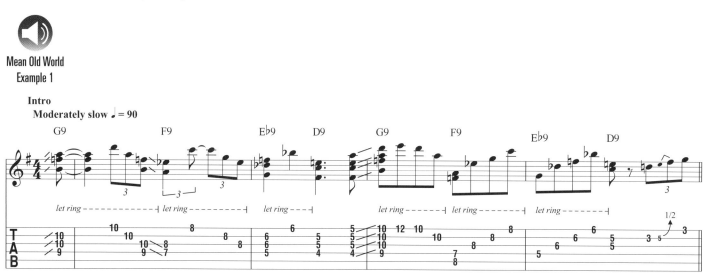

Performance Tip: Though Walker does not pick all five notes of each chord, it makes good sense to hold the complete fingering throughout (see photo).

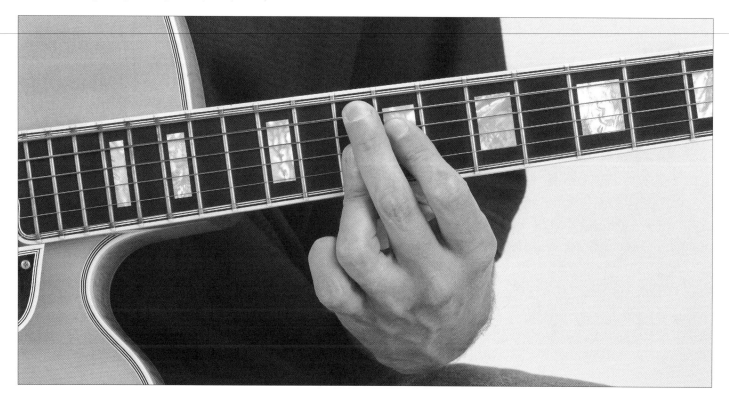

Guitar Solo

Walker virtually "lived" in the root position of the composite blues scale. Combining choice notes from the blues scale and the Mixolydian mode, he enjoyed his time there in measures 5–16.

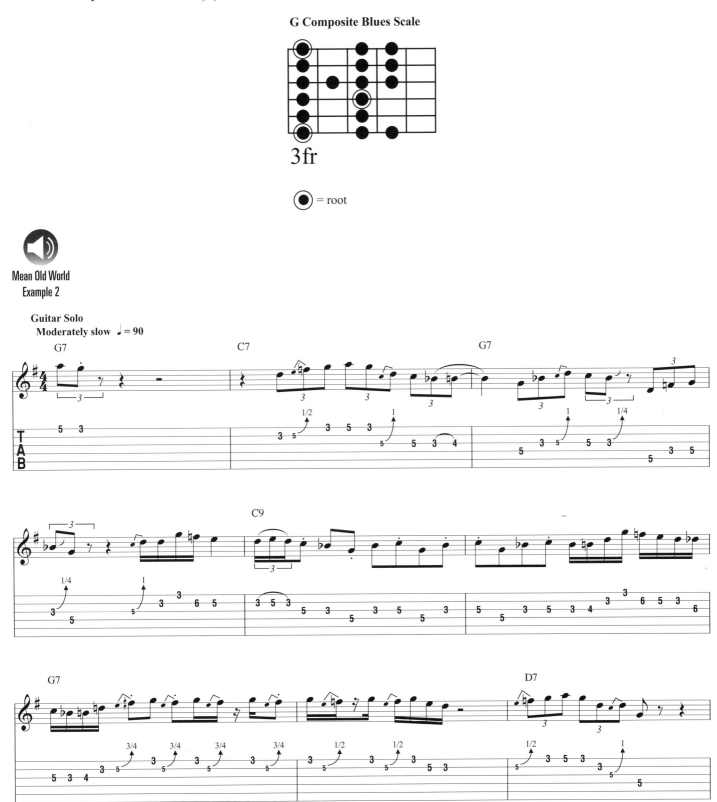

G Composite Blues Scale

3fr

● = root

Mean Old World
Example 2

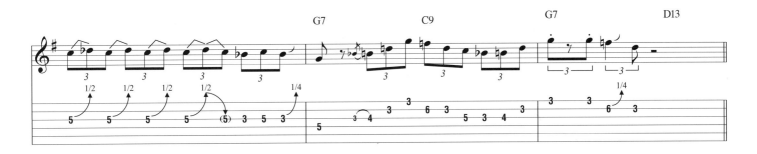

Even a casual listen reveals subtle chord change navigation, particularly from the I (G) to the IV (C7). The "secret" lies in simple emphasis on the "target notes" of both chords.

The target notes of the I chord (G) are: root (G), 5th (D), and ♭7th (F).

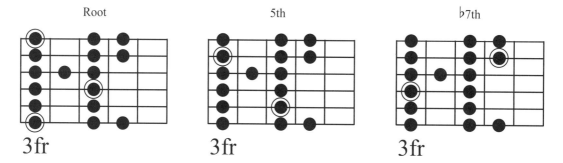

The target notes of the IV chord (C7) are: root (C), major 3rd (E), and 5th (G).

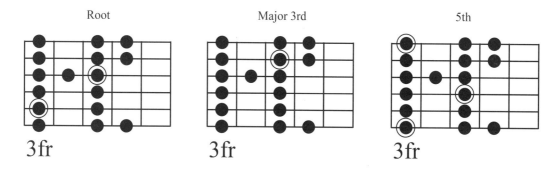

Performance Tip: These signature Walker licks contain the major 3rd (B) of the I chord (G), as seen in measures 11 and 15. Presence of the major 3rd is the number one method of confirming the major tonality of a chord.

Mean Old World
Example 3

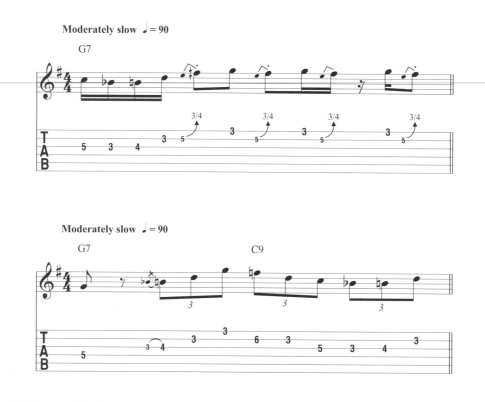

Performance Tip: Walker mainly fretted with his index and ring fingers, most often bending by pushing up with his ring finger on strings 3 and 2.

Measure 11 features a classic T-Bone bending lick. He uses a bend over the I chord (G), which sums up the basis of blues soloing: the creation of musical tension followed by release. In this case, the root (G) is spiced with the 6th (E) bent 3/4 step to a gnarly micro-tone between the ♭7th (F) and major 7th (F♯), repeated for maximum power.

Performance Tip: Over the I chord (G) in measure 12, Walker bends the 6th (E) one half step to the ♭7th (F), thereby implying the dominant quality of the chord change (see photo).

Mean Old World
Example 4

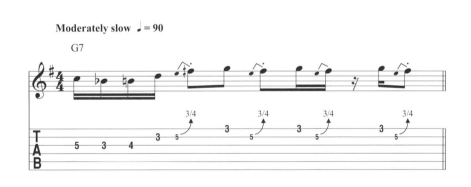

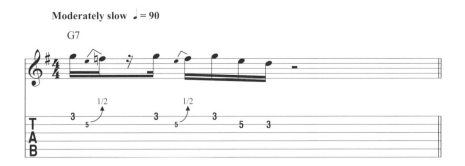

Measures 17–28, the second chorus of blues, find Walker taking a totally different tact by building tart tension in measures 17–19 over the I–IV–I changes. Abandoning his typical root position and relocating to the 10th position of the G blues scale, he announces his presence and traditional blues cred with the classic, iconic "train whistle." Few blues licks are as evocative.

Performance Tip: Place the index finger on string 1 at fret 10 (D) and bend string 2 at fret 11 (Bb) with the middle finger.

Observe how Walker resolves the tension over the I chord in measure 20 with a strummed 9th-position G9 chord. Blending scale tones and chords is a stylistic characteristic indicative of Walker's jazz influences.

Mean Old World
Example 5

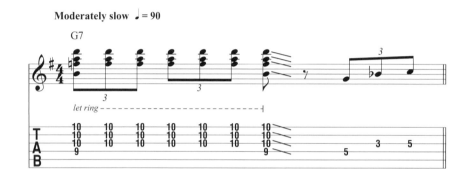

Measure 25 presents the composite blues scale in all its glory. Target notes within the snappy 16th-note licks include: the b7th (G) and 5th (E) of an implied ii chord (Am7), and the root (D) and 5th (A) of the V chord (D7). Moving from a ii chord to a V chord to a I chord is extremely common in jazz.

Performance Tip: Notice the four consecutive notes on string 3 across beats 2 and 3. This fluid, chromatic effect is rare in the blues, but again, typical of much jazz.

Mean Old World
Example 6

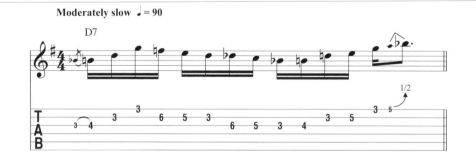

Verse 3

The final Verse finds Walker punctuating the chilling lyrics with one of his most iconic rhythm riffs. In measures 55–56, 59–60, and 63–64, he repeatedly bends a G°7 triad a quarter or half step on strings 3–1 (see photo), creating stunning musical tension over the I chord (G). The result almost literally "stops time," only to be restarted in the resolving measures that follow.

Performance Tip: Finger the diminished 7th triad as if playing a first-position D7 chord: middle, index, and ring, low to high (see photo).

Mean Old World
Example 7

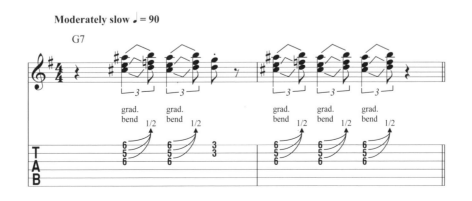

MEAN OLD WORLD
Words and Music by Aaron "T-Bone" Walker

Mean Old World
Full Song

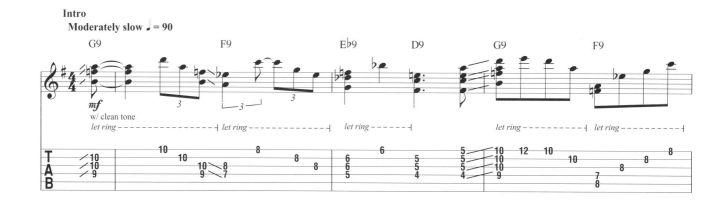

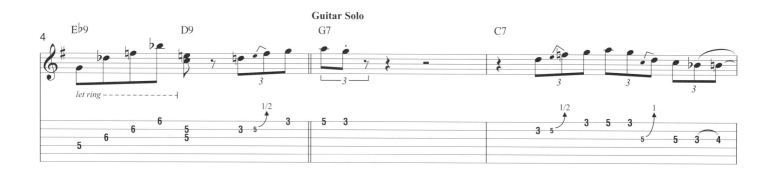

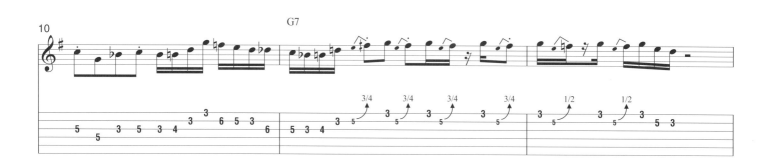

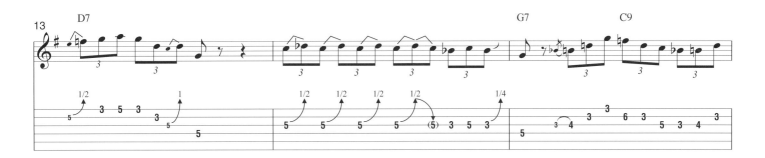

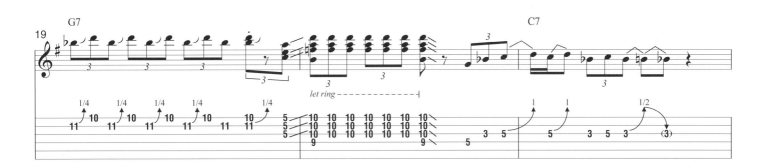

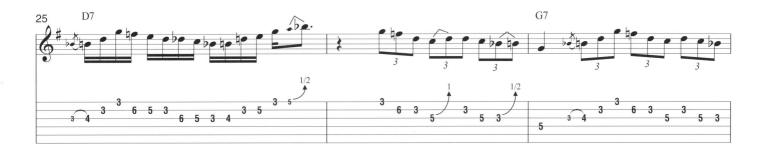

Verse

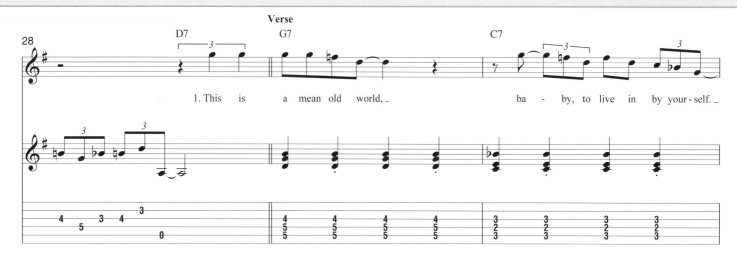

1. This is a mean old world, _ ba - by, to live in by your - self. _

_ This is a mean old world, _ babe, _

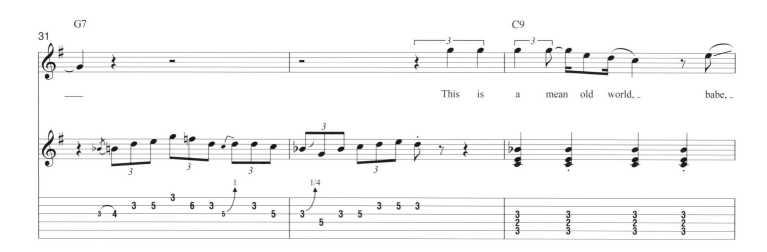

_ to _ live in by your - self. _ When you can't _

let ring *let ring* *let ring*

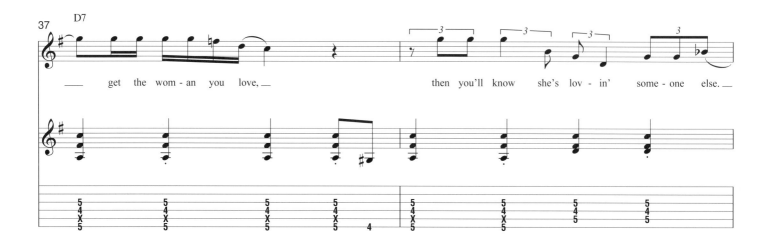

_ get the wom - an you love, _ then you'll know she's lov - in' some - one else. _

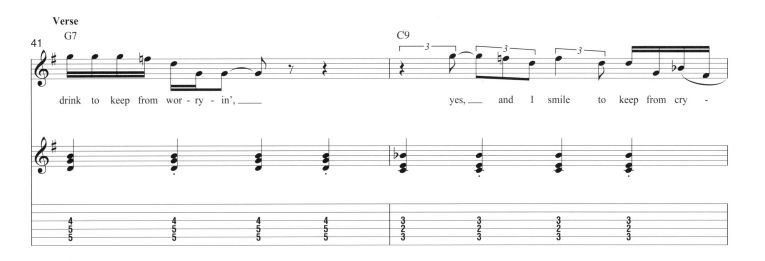

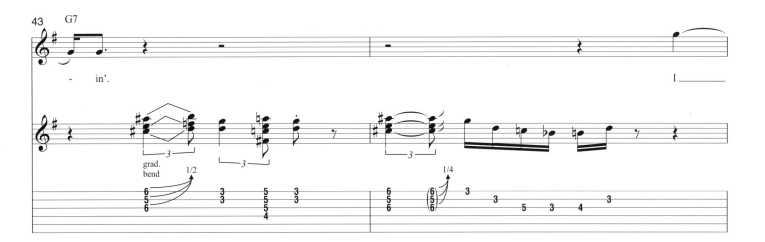

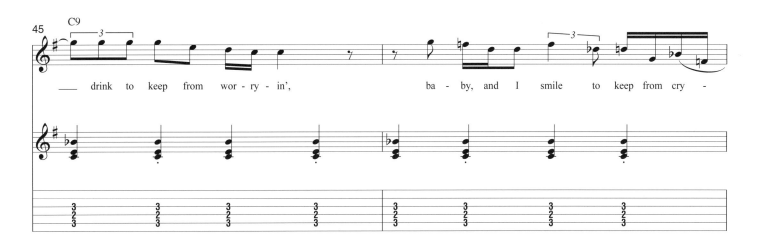

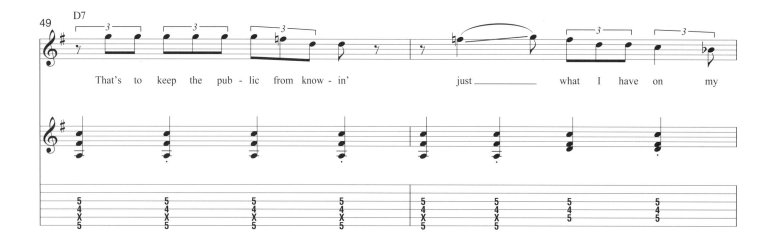

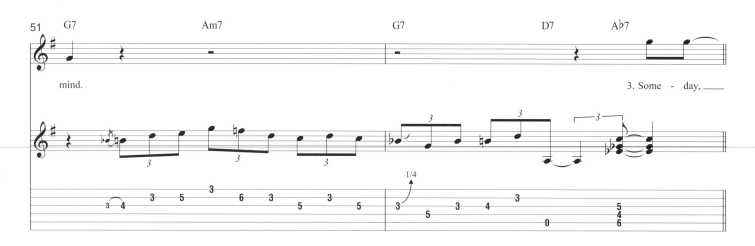

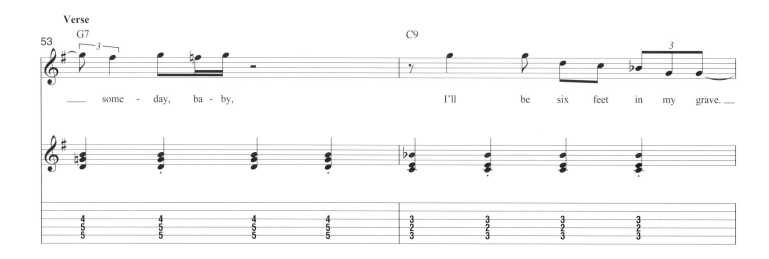

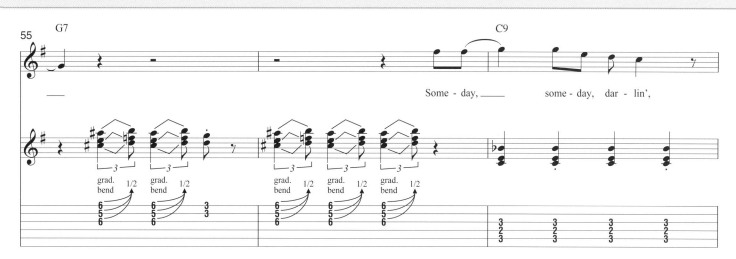

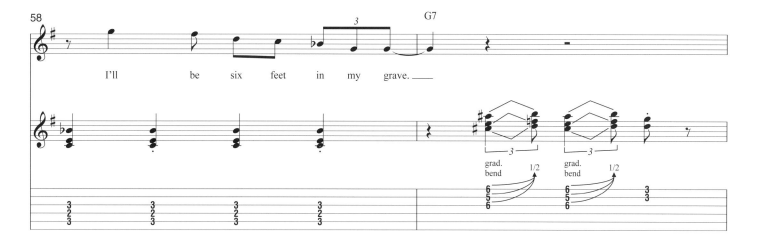

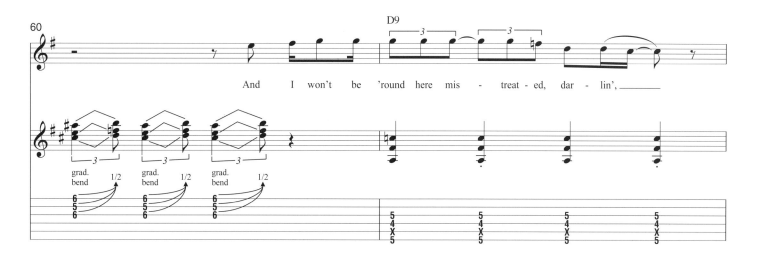

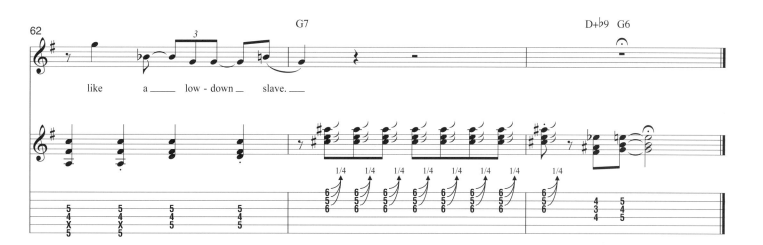

I Got a Break Baby (1942)
From *T-Bone Walker: The Ultimate Collection 1929–57*

"I Got a Break Baby," paired with "Mean Old World," delivered a one-two punch to the ears of other electric blues and jazz guitarists in the 1940s. These two benchmarks of pre-war electric blues debuted Walker as a fully formed exponent of what would come to be recognized and lauded as the touchstone for virtually all electric guitar to follow.

Intro

Though recorded at the same session as "Mean Old World," "I Got a Break Baby" shows even more advanced improvisation in the two-chorus Intro. Not to be overlooked is the smooth, "ebony" sound of the (possibly) ES-250, not unlike the midrange of a clarinet. The vast richness of his melodies and harmonies more than makes up for the fact that the song does not contain a solo.

Pay attention to the way Walker emphasizes the major 3rd (E) of the I chord (C9) on string 3 in measures 1 (where it is bent up to from the ♭3rd), 4, 7, and 11. Conversely, in measures 2, 5, and 6, he highlights the ♭7th (E♭) and root (F) of the IV chord (F9) on string 3 at frets 8 and 10, respectively. In measures 9–10, he focuses on the root (G) of the V chord (G9) on string 2 at fret 8, in addition to fret 10 on string 5.

Performance Tip: The proximity of the notes is one of the prime advantages of the root position of the composite blues scale. In measures 9–10, a dramatic relocation to the bass strings for an ascending run adds an element of drama.

I Got a Break Baby
    Example 1

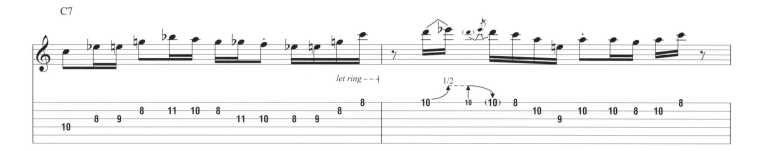

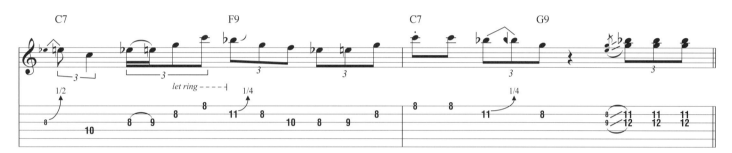

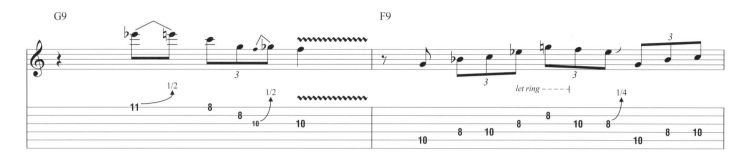

Setting the stage for Chuck Berry in the 1950s, as well as countless other blues and rock guitarists, Walker comes romping into the second blues chorus with the ♭7th (B♭) and 5th (G) of the I chord (C9). In measures 13–15, this repetitive dyad is phrased in triplets and indicates C dominant tonality. The blast of propulsive energy is intelligently and aesthetically reined in with C9/E and C#9/F "jazz voicings" in measure 16, before the crafty change to the IV chord (F9).

Performance Tip: Observe how measures 1–12 contain the "fast change" from I–IV while measures 13–24 include the "slow change." Consequently, Walker navigates the chords accordingly.

I Got a Break Baby
Example 2

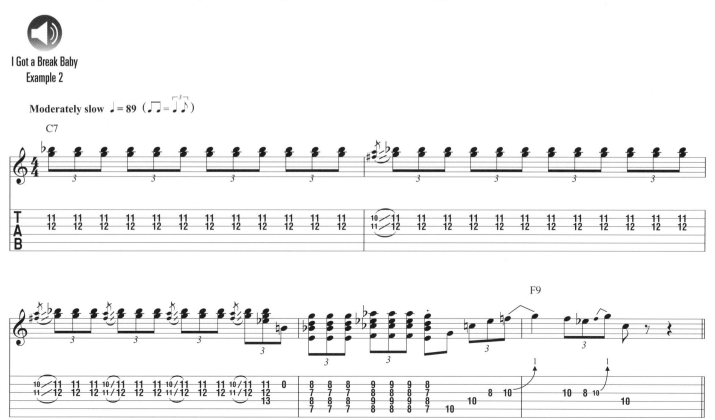

Played over both the IV chord (F9) and the I chord (C9), measures 18 and 19 feature the first appearance on record of a Walker signature lick involving the F on string 3 bent one step to G, followed by the fretted G on string 2. It cannot be confirmed if he was literally the inventor of the pugnacious lick (*Note*: Walker was known to be a scrapper), but Chuck Berry clearly appropriated it to great success for classics like "Johnny B. Goode."

Performance Tip: Anchor the index finger on string 2 and bend string 3 with the ring finger backed up by the middle finger (see photo).

I Got a Break Baby
Example 3

*Played as even eighth notes.

Measures 31–32 offer a perfect example of a signature Walker turnaround in the root position of the composite blues scale. The triplet on beat 2 of measure 31, with the push-off bend on string 3, is "Electric Blues Guitar 101."

Performance Tip: Bend the F on string 3 with the ring finger as the index holds down strings 2 and 1. On beat 4 of measure 31, pull *down* with the index finger to bend the E♭.

I Got a Break Baby
Example 4

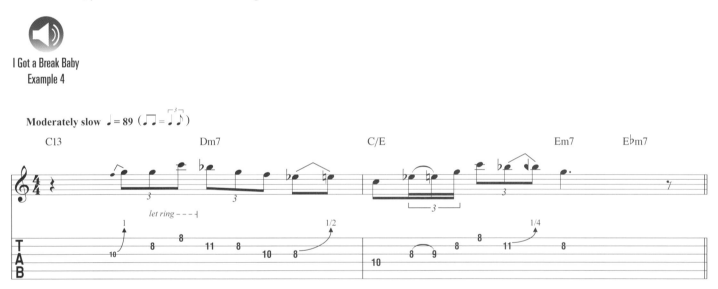

Verse 3

Though rightly revered as a master purveyor of elegant and assertive single-note lines, Walker also knew how to manipulate chordal riffs to stunning effect. In measures 51–52 and 55–56, he follows his vocal line by combining a gritty implied C°7 chord with an implied C major and F6 chord for a brilliantly harmonized blues riff over the I chord (C9).

Performance Tip: Efficient fingering should always be one of the goals of a guitar player no matter the style of music. It is a maxim nowhere more apparent than here. Play the diminished chord, low to high, with the middle, index, and ring fingers, realizing that rather than aiming for an exact pitch, the multi-string bend is more of a "feel thing." Nick the C-G dyad with the index finger as a small barre and catch the F6 with the ring finger as a barre.

I Got a Break Baby
   Example 5

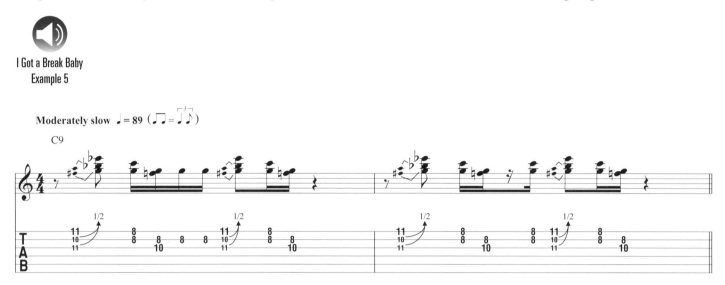

Verse 4

Walker was clearly not the first guitarist to play diminished chords, but he *may* have been the first to bend them! In measures 63, 64, 67, and 68, he creates exquisite musical tension by repeatedly bending the C°7 chord over the I chord.

In measure 72, Walker introduces one of his signature chord voicings: a first-inversion 9th chord with the 3rd on the bottom. As shown, it is particularly expressive when "organically" moved to the I chord from one half step above.

Performance Tip: Low to high, finger this chord shape using your index, ring, middle, and pinky fingers.

I Got a Break Baby
   Example 6

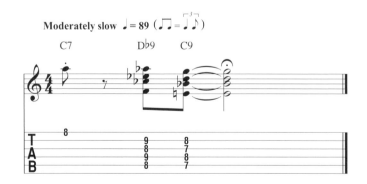

I GOT A BREAK BABY

Words and Music by Aaron Walker

I Got a Break Baby
Full Song

*Chord symbols reflect implied harmony.

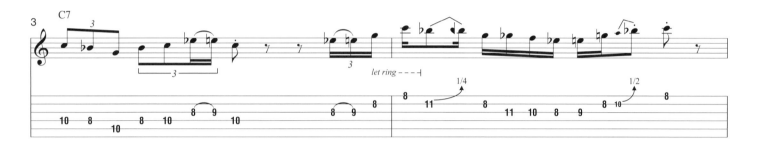

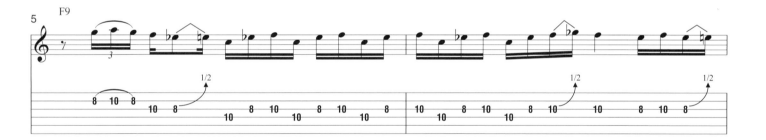

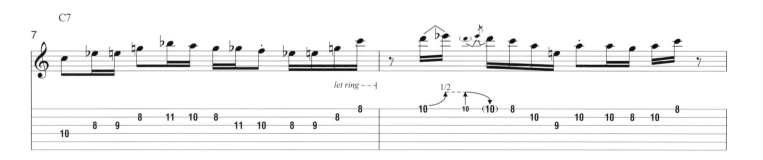

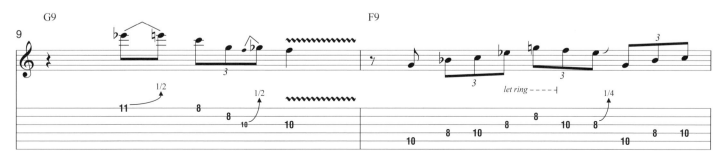

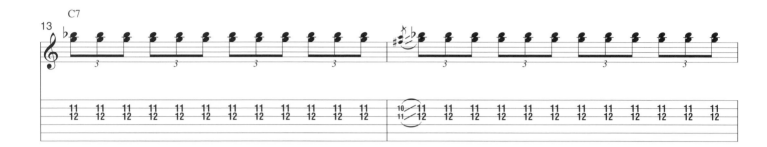

*Played as even eighth notes.

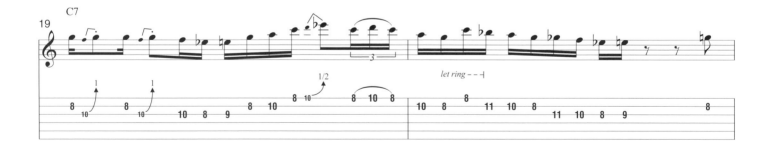

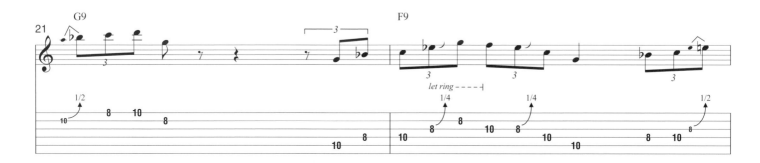

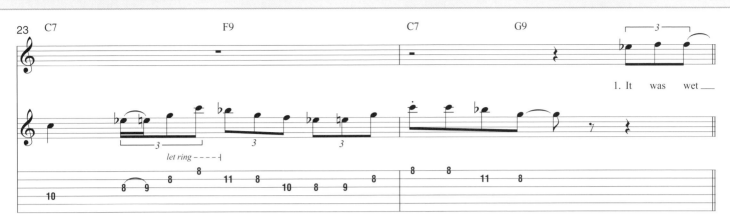

Verse

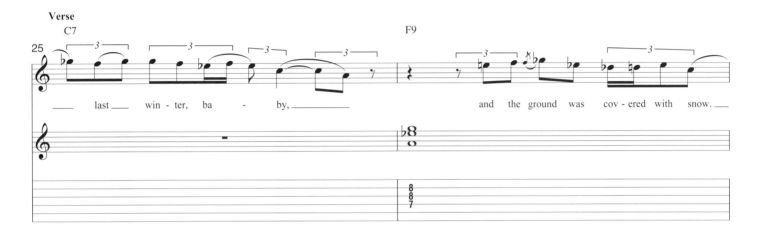

Gtr. tacet

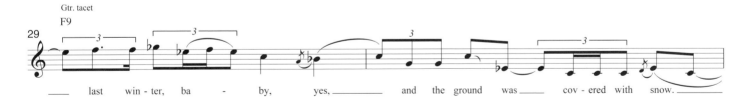

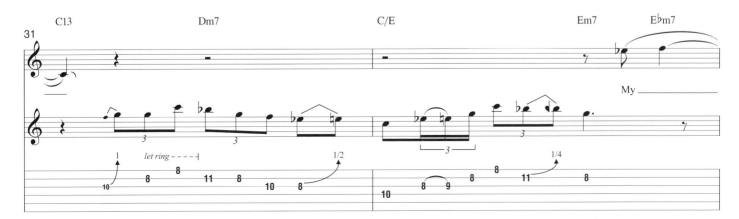

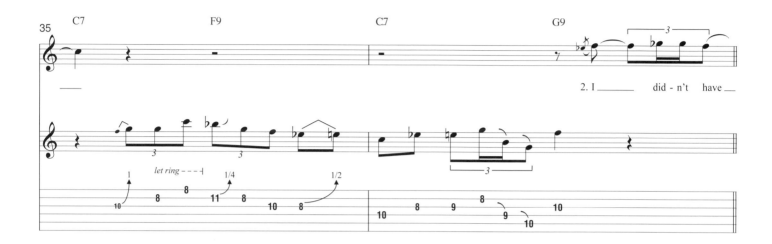

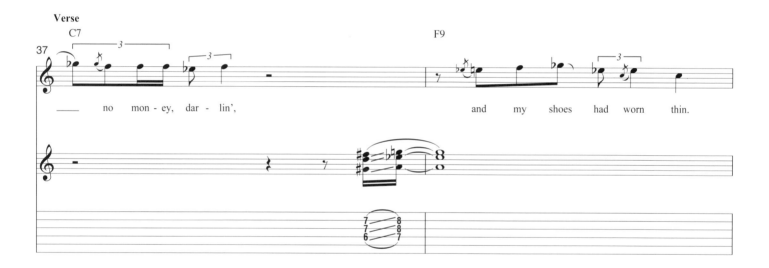

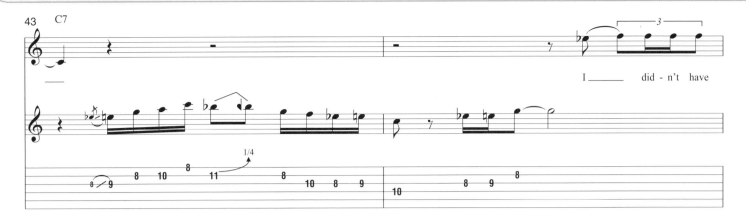

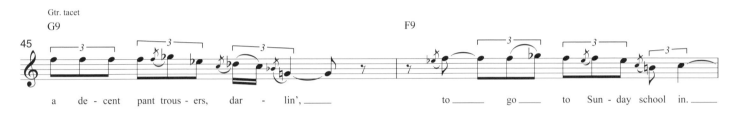

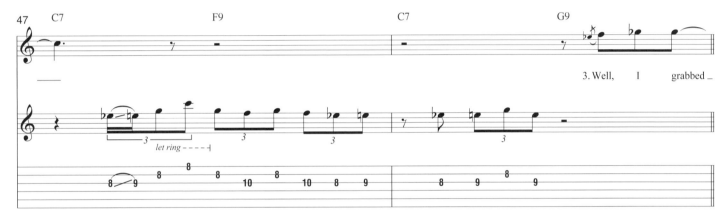

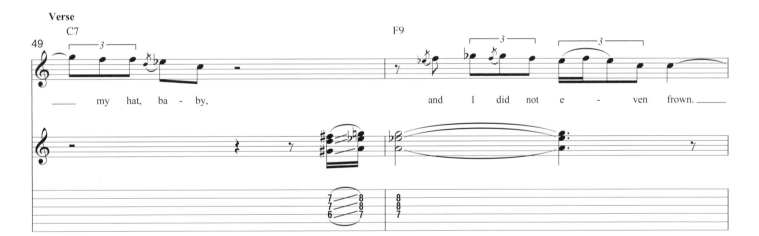

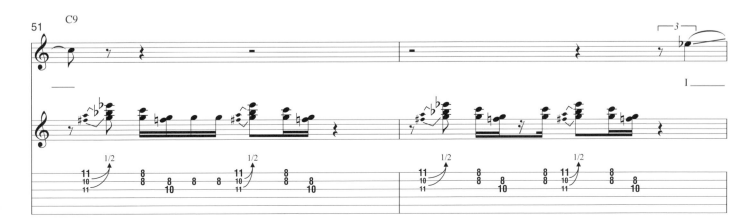

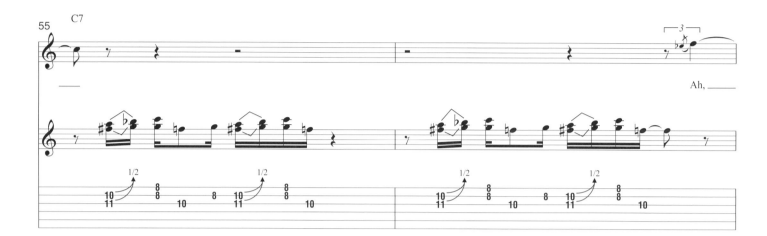

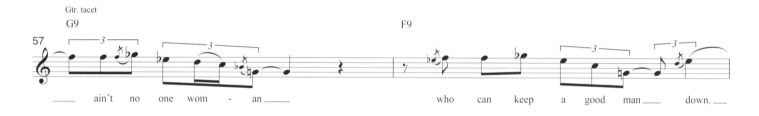

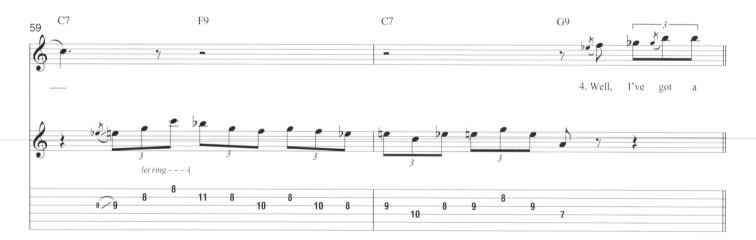

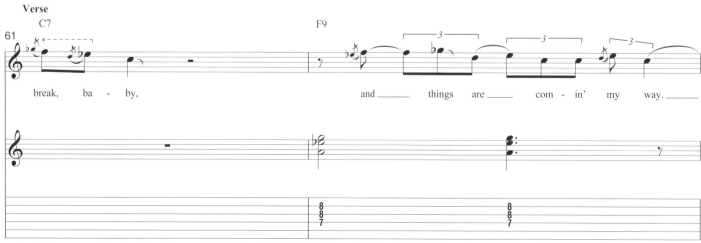

*Sung as even eighth notes.

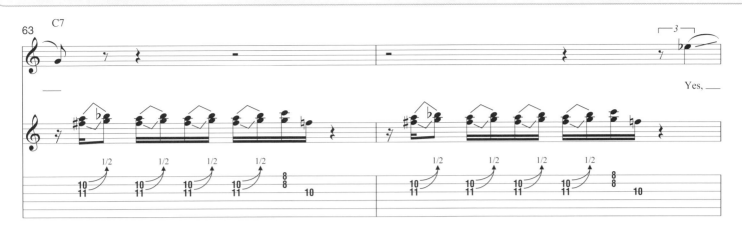

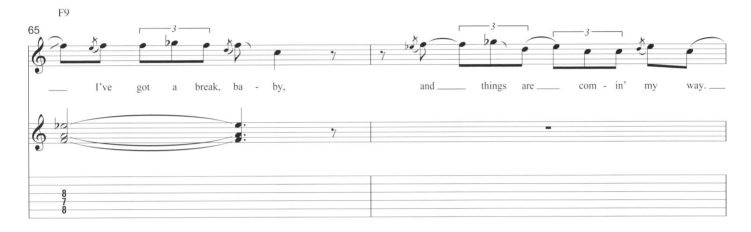

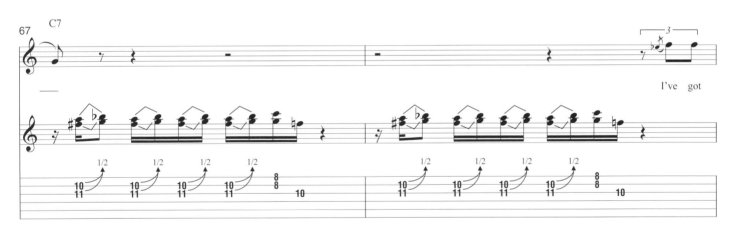

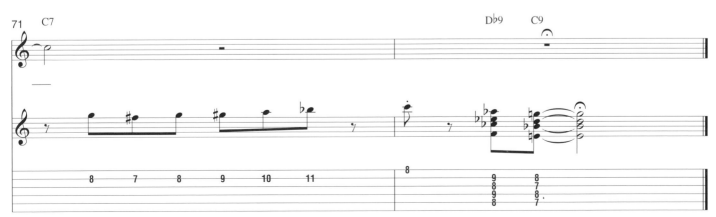

(They Call It) Stormy Monday (Stormy Monday Blues) (1947, #5 R&B)
From *Blues Masters: The Very Best of T-Bone Walker* (Rhino)

Controversy surrounds the exact recording date of the acknowledged number one slow blues standard of all time. Despite the official 1947 release date, Walker claimed that he cut it "before the war (World War II)" but a shortage of shellac during the war years held it up. Unfortunately, jazz singer Billy Eckstine recorded a song called "Stormy Monday" in 1942—a completely different song in which the words "Stormy Monday" do not even appear. "Call It Stormy Monday (Tuesday Is Just as Bad)" was Walker's complete original title, so named to differentiate it from the Eckstine recording. Still, it would go on to be constantly mixed up with the other song, resulting in a great loss of royalties to the electric guitar genius. Nonetheless, it did contribute to his fame and he subsequently recorded other versions. However, most contemporary blues guitarists look back to the Allman Brothers Band's live version from 1971, built on the 1962 Bobby Blue Bland version featuring Wayne Bennett and his numerous sliding 6/9 chords and other substitutions.

Intro

Instead of a standard V7–I turnaround, Walker often chose to use a #V7–V7–I turnaround. In the key of G, this would be Eb7–D7–G.

Performance Tip: Since there's not a guitar part written out for the Intro, check out this additional transcription created from the horn and piano parts. Not many guitarists would opt to play it exactly like that, but it will go far in pumping up your blues guitar cred!

Stormy Monday
Example 1

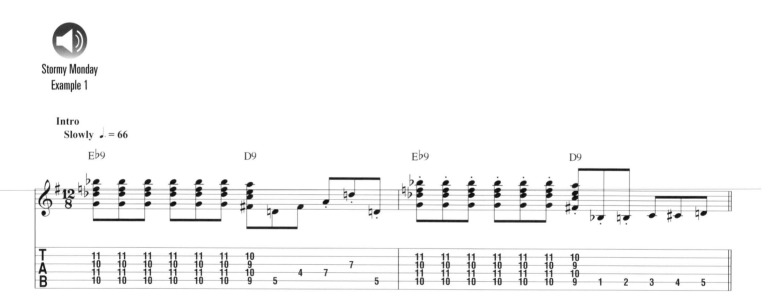

Verse 1

Measures 9 and 10 contain classic Walker moveable 9th chords, beloved by and gladly assimilated into the playing of generations of blues guitarists. This two-measure fill works over the I chord during the third and fourth measures (or the seventh and eighth measures) of a basic 12-bar blues form.

Performance Tip: In Verse 1, notice how only measures 7 and 8 include his signature moveable 9ths. In Verse 2, however, Walker is more generous with the chordal riff, using slight variations of it in measures 3 and 4, and again in measures 7 and 8.

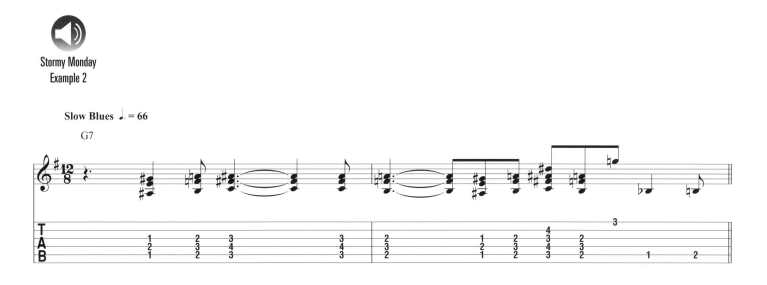

Stormy Monday
Example 2

Guitar Solo

As he did so many times throughout his long, G-string-bending career, Walker convincingly proves how protean the root position of the composite blues scale can be in the hands of a creative guitarist. In measures 27–30, he mainly relies on the tension-inducing bend of the 4th (C) to the 5th (D) of the I chord (G6), resolving to the root (C) of the IV chord (C9). However, beginning on beat 4 of measure 30 and continuing through measures 31 and 32, he alternates a lick that moves from the 3rd (E) to the root (C) to the ♭7th (B♭) of the IV chord (C9), with another that moves from the 3rd (E) to the root (C) to the 6th (A) of the IV chord (C9), producing a harmonious musical tapestry against the voicing. A repeated pattern like this can also serve as a "bridge" between two sections of fluid single-note runs.

Performance Tip: Slide into the 3rd (E) with the middle finger, followed by the index for the root (C) and the pinky for the ♭7th. Use the ring finger for the 6th (A).

A master at connecting chord changes, Walker transposes the previous lick containing the 3rd (E), the root (C), and the ♭7th (B♭) to fit the I chord (G7) in measure 33 (beginning on beat 3 1/2 of measure 32). From there, on through to the end of the solo, single-note lines flow like Texas oil, with some intelligent choices well worth acknowledging…

In measure 35, he bends the 9th (E) of the V chord (D7) to the ♯9th (F) of the V chord (D7) to lend tart tension to beats 1 and 2. A D7♯9 chord would naturally sound good over this measure because of the prominent ♯9 (F) the chord contains.

In measure 36, where one would expect to encounter the IV chord (C9), Walker repeats the V chord (D7). And just to make sure no one overlooks it, he bends the ♭7th (C) of the V chord (D7) to the root (D) of the V chord (D7) twice, while also emphasizing the ♭7th (C) of the V chord (D7) several times as a complement to the D dominant harmony.

The turnaround in measures 37 and 38 does not "turn around" via the V chord (D7) as one would generally expect. Instead, Walker maintains forward momentum by repeating the I chord (G7) and smartly crafting a lick in the key of G running from root (G) to root (G). Finally, in measure 38, he finishes up on the higher of the two roots (G) found in the lick, further reinforcing the drive into the I chord (G9) in the next Verse (not shown).

Stormy Monday
Example 3

Guitar Solo
Slow Blues ♩ = 66

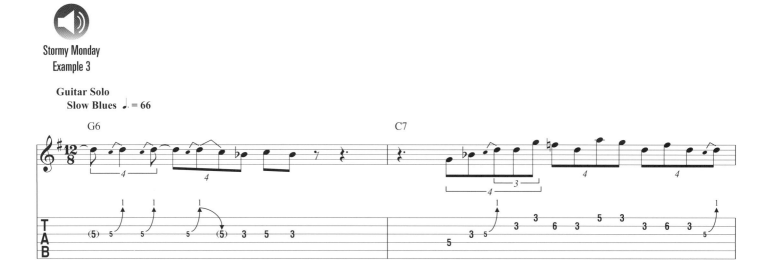

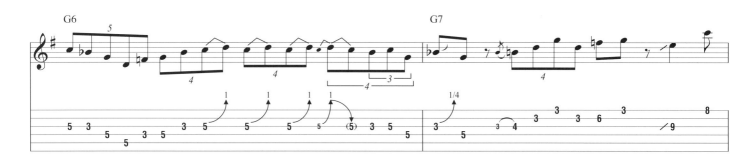

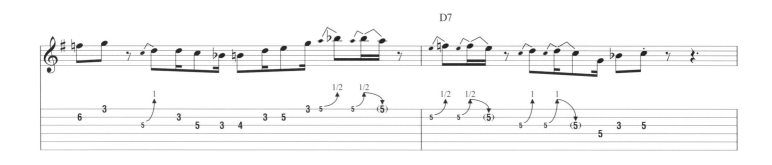

(THEY CALL IT) STORMY MONDAY
(STORMY MONDAY BLUES)

Words and Music by Aaron "T-Bone" Walker

Stormy Monday
Full Song

Wednes - day's worse, ___ and ___ Thurs - day's al - so sad. ___

___ 2. Yes, _____

Verse

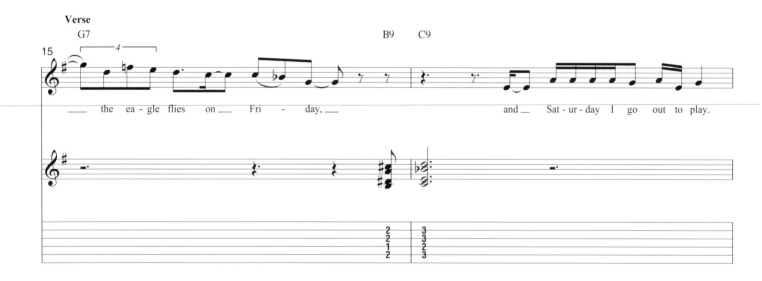

___ the ea - gle flies on ___ Fri - day, ___ and __ Sat - ur - day I go out to play.

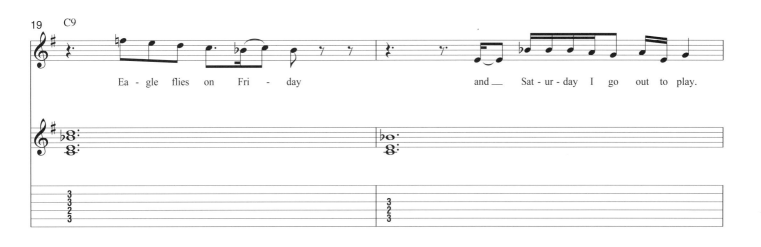

Ea - gle flies on Fri - day and ___ Sat - ur - day I go out to play.

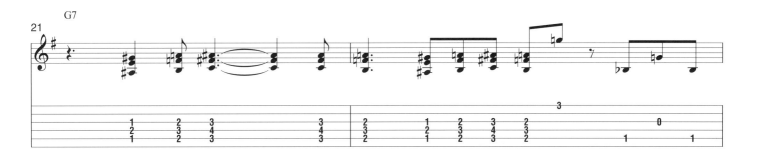

Sun - day I go to church, then I ___ kneel ___ down and

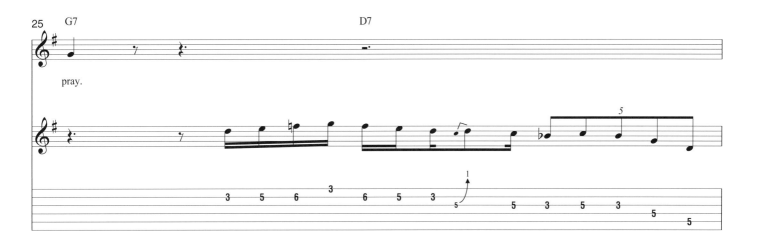

pray.

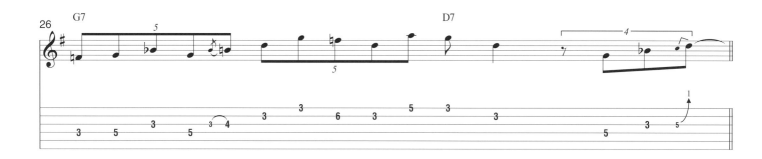

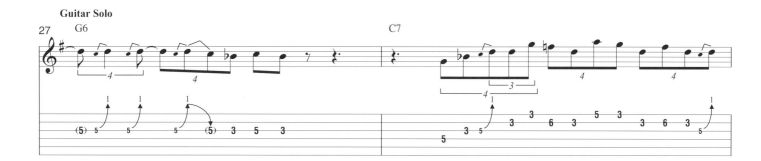

Guitar Solo

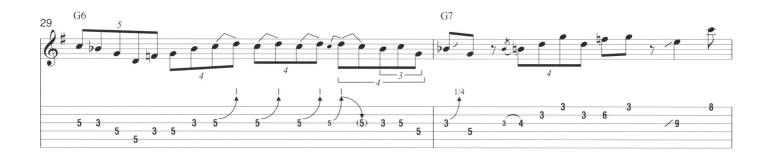

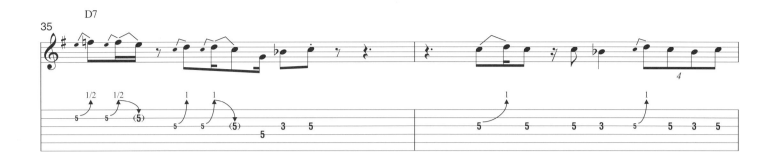

Verse

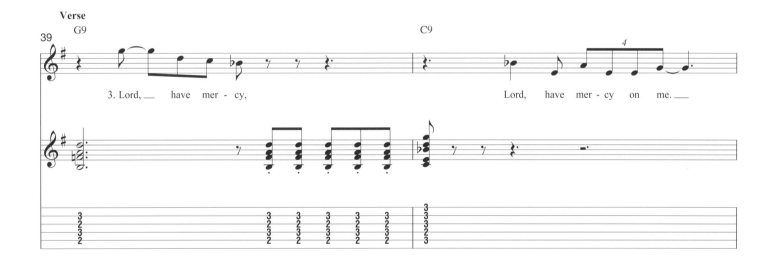

3. Lord, ___ have mer - cy,   Lord,   have mer - cy on me. ___

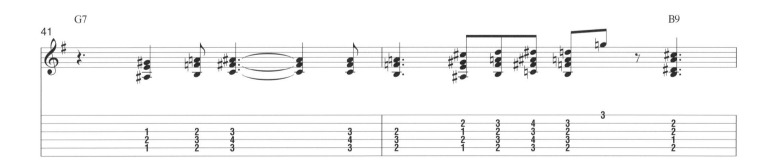

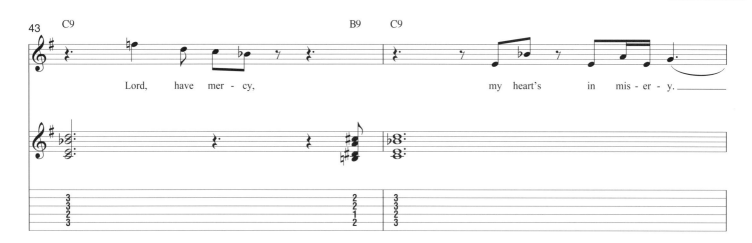

Lord, have mer - cy, my heart's in mis - er - y.

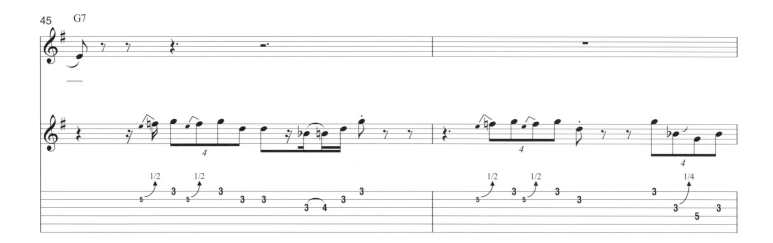

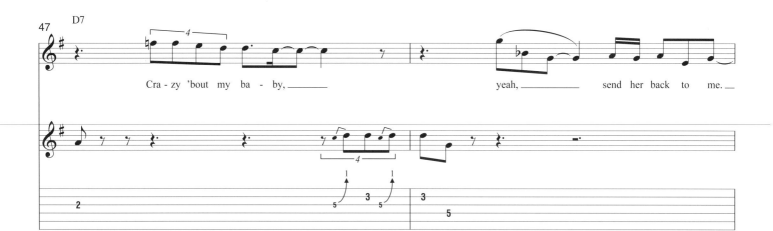

Cra - zy 'bout my ba - by, yeah, send her back to me.

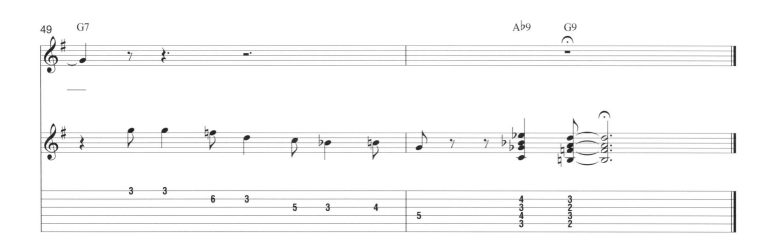

T-Bone Shuffle (1947)
From *Blues Masters: The Very Best of T-Bone Walker*

"There's nothing wrong with you that a good shuffle boogie won't cure."
–T-Bone Walker

Released in the era of swing *and* bebop, "T-Bone Shuffle" shows more than a little relationship to jazz; the arrangement features extensive improvisation within 12-bar sections that alternate between vocals and saxophone, guitar, and trumpet solos. The instrumental "head" is deceptively simple, but is a favorite of blues guitarists, nonetheless. One of the best-known versions was released in 1985 on the Grammy-winning *Showdown!* (Alligator Records), featuring Albert Collins, Robert Cray, and Johnny Copeland. It is a great one to have in your repertoire for jamming. And a quick learn to boot!

Intro

The four-measure boogie woogie piano part preceding the head sets the irresistible groove. It has been transcribed for guitar, and as you can see, the key of G naturally lends itself to the concept. The open-string dyads may be thought of as the right-hand piano part, while the walking bass line created by the notes on the downbeats represents a pianist's left hand. Boogie woogie piano played on the guitar is a treat, builds new technique, and has many applications in blues and rock music.

Performance Tip: Create a shortened open G "folk guitar" shape with your left hand, using the ring and middle fingers. This way, the index finger is free to access the E note on string 4 at fret 2. Be aware, the most efficient right-hand technique is playing fingerstyle with the thumb and index fingers, or hybrid picking (pick and fingers). However, a real flat-picking challenge awaits if that is the chosen course. Either way, pluck or pick down on the bass strings and up on strings 2 and 3.

T-Bone Shuffle
Example 1

*Piano arr. for gtr.

Head

The basic curriculum from the "Less Is More School of Blues" is on full display to produce a timeless 12-bar blues head in two-measure increments. Walker employs the root-position G minor pentatonic scale with the addition of the crucial major 3rd (B). Essentially, he begins each measure of the I chord (G) with the tonality-defining major 3rd (B), each time following the pickup notes of G and B♭ heard on the "and" of beat 3. Measures 9 and 10 commence with the ♭3rd (B♭) of the I chord (G), now functioning as the ♭7th of the IV chord (C7).

Having decided to use just two two-measure phrases throughout, Walker had to choose which one to play over the V chord (D7). His solution? Simply repeat the same two-measure phrase he played over the I chord (G), starting with the G and B♭ in measure 12. The target note (B) in measure 13 now functions as the major 6th of the V chord (D7), and in measure 14, it functions as the *major* 7th of the IV chord (C7)! It may not be funky, down-home blues harmony, but theoretically it is perfectly acceptable. Measures 15–16 quite naturally receive the two-measure pattern played over the I chord (G), though slightly altered in order to resolve conclusively on the B note.

Performance Tip: The two-measure riff is compact with the notes conveniently placed. In each riff, use the ring finger for the G and C notes at fret 5. Use the middle finger for the B note at fret 4 and the index finger for the D note at fret 3.

T-Bone Shuffle
Example 2

Intro
Moderately ♩ = 140

Guitar Solo

Walker appears to be far enough behind the beat to be staring into the taillights of his rhythm section. Though it is actually a musical mirage, his relaxed phrasing does produce a really hypnotic effect on the listener. His intuitive use of dynamic musical space in the first chorus teaches a lesson that cannot be emphasized enough for contemporary blues guitarists who tend to fill every nook and cranny of a measure when soloing.

Walker was obviously not the first blues guitarist to bend the 4th (C) of the I chord (G) on string 3 at fret 5, but he seems to get more musical mileage out of it than most others. To the point, he bends it up one step seven times in the first chorus of blues alone!

Performance Tip: Check out how Walker often follows the G-string bend to D with the fretted D note on string 2, a patented move with which he seems to "slow" time even further (see photo).

Walker immediately ramps up the energy quotient in the second chorus of blues with three dramatic measures of bending. He bends the ♭3rd (B♭) of the I chord (G) a quarter step to the "true blue note" (in between the ♭3rd and major 3rd) on each downbeat. The musical tension created is truly palpable and further accentuated with slippery descending triplets in measure 56. Rather than continuing powerful propulsion into the IV chord (C7), however, Walker shifts his soloing tact with almost two full measures of laconic, descending scale notes before halting the dynamic contrast with a bend from the root (C) of the IV chord (C7) to the ♭5th (D♭) of the I chord (G) across the bar line.

Walker caps the previous six measures with a relaxed combination of notes and bends that end on the 5th (D) of the I chord (G). He rests dramatically at the end of measure 59 through the beginning of measure 60 before relying on the classic unison bend (as seen in the Performance Tip above) into measure 61 of the V chord (D7). The musical tension swells into measures 63 and 64 where the I chord maintains momentum into Verse 2 as Walker floats over the chords like an eagle.

T-Bone Shuffle
Example 3

Guitar Solo
Moderately ♩ = 140

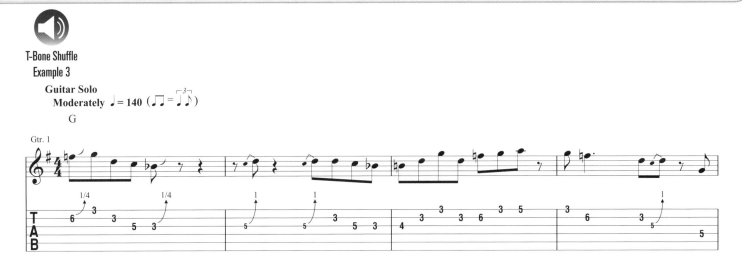

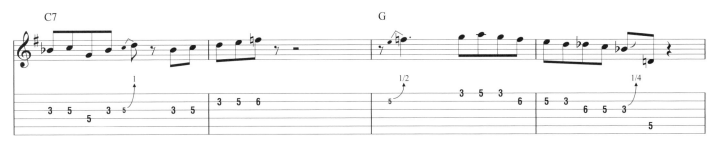

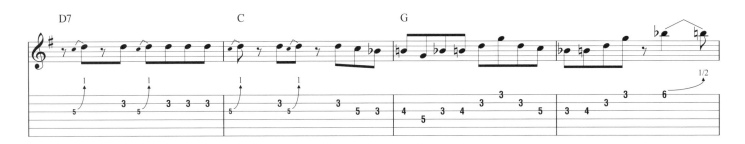

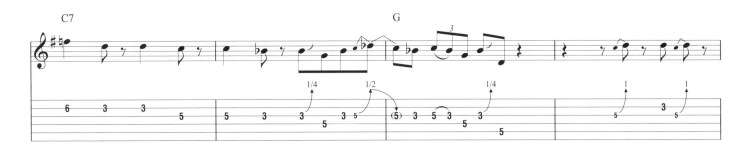

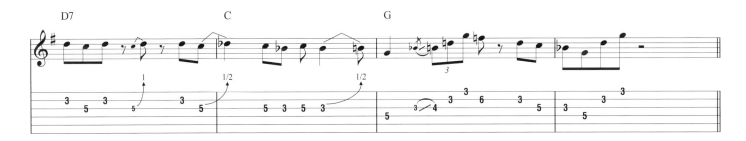

T-BONE SHUFFLE

By T-Bone Walker

T-Bone Shuffle
Full Song

Guitar Solo

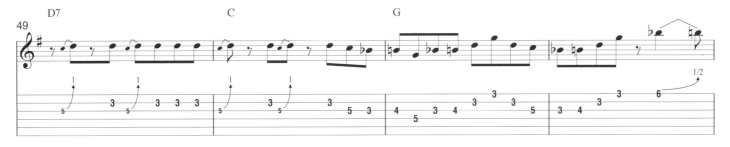

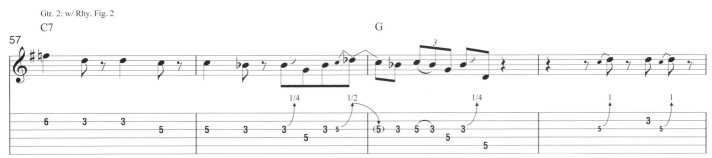

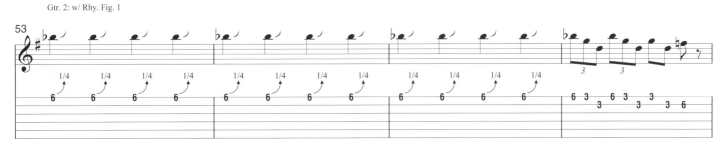

D.S. al Coda

2. You can't _

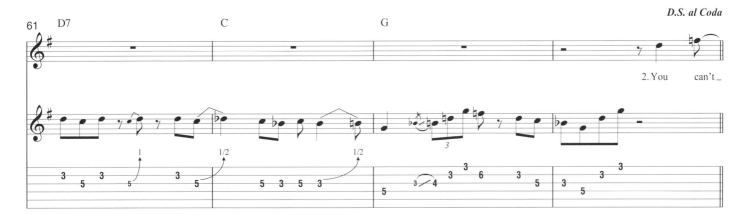

Coda 1

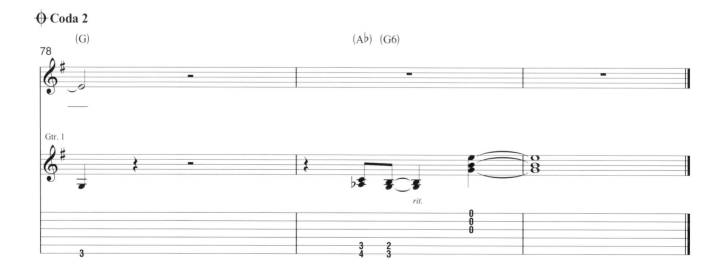

Coda 2

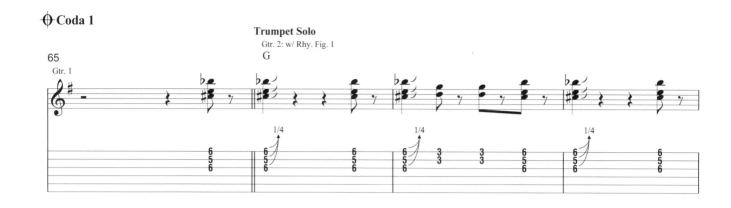

Strollin' with Bones (1950)

From *The Complete Imperial Recordings: 1950–1954*

This performance of "Strollin' with Bones" is not only one of the greatest, most virtuosic of T-Bone Walker's unexcelled career, but also is one of the most hard-charging swing blues instrumentals in history. His phrasing and technique are flawless, the dynamics are explosive, and the barreling steam locomotive energy presages rock 'n' roll in this centerpiece of his oeuvre.

Section B

The "call and response" between the horns and Walker's guitar in Letter B (serving as the "head") finds him locked into the groove like the transmission of a 1947 Cadillac LaSalle in high gear. By measure 8, he is clearly in the driver's seat, cruising from Central Avenue to Sunset Boulevard in Los Angeles. Observe his use of the Eb functioning as the root and the Db as the b7th to define the change to the IV chord (Eb9). In measure 10, he aptly demonstrates how to create bluesy musical tension by combining the 5th (F), b5th (E), 4th (Eb), and b3rd (Db) of the I chord (Bb7) into a descending line. In the same measure, resolution to the I chord (Bb7) tonality arrives courtesy of an upward move to the major 3rd (D), the 5th (F), and the root (Bb) with suave élan.

Strollin' with Bones
Example 1

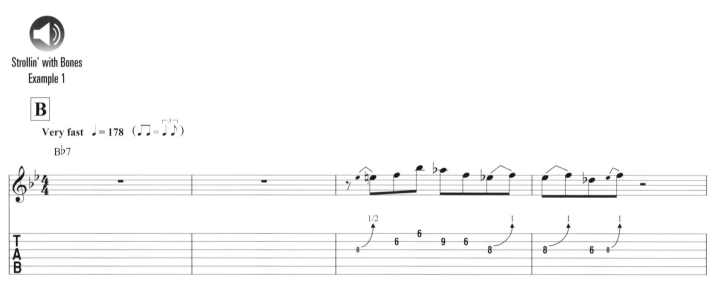

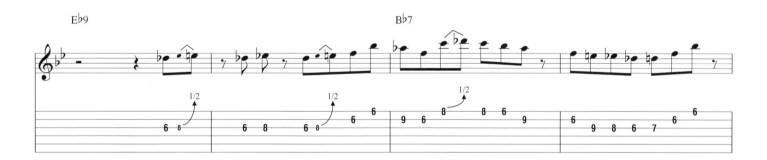

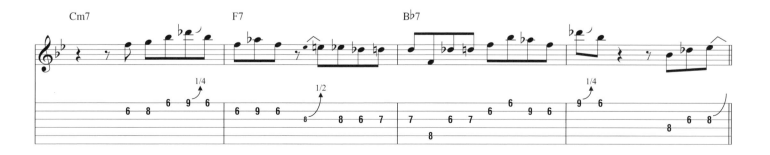

Though not duplicated by Walker, the swinging signature horn riff is well worth knowing by guitarists and may efficiently be played in the root position of the B♭ composite blues scale. Since there are at least five beats of rest following each repetitive two-measure riff, there is still plenty of musical space for improvising in a call-and-response manner.

Performance Tip: Observe how the exact same notes harmonize over the I (B♭7), IV (E♭9), and ii–V (Cm7–F7) chord changes. It is a great example of the marvelous melodic flexibility of the composite blues scale, and variations can be found in many blues classics.

Strollin' with Bones
Example 2

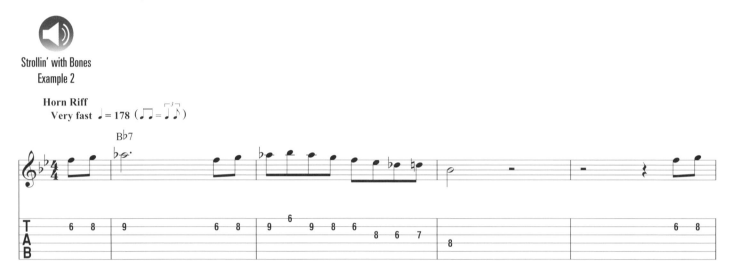

Section E

Not to wear out the car metaphor, but Walker smoothly accelerates from chorus to chorus of blues. In Letter E, he lays down a soloing strategy for composing a magnificent 12-bar improvisation which blues guitarists would do well to heed. He starts out at a conservative pace in the four measures of the I chord (Bb7), with dramatic musical space and gently propulsive bends. However, over the IV chord (Eb9) and I chord (Bb7) in measures 43–45, he gives it the gas with twisting, repetitive licks involving three notes, including quarter-step bends to the "true blue note" between Db and D.

Cruising to the ii7 chord (Cm7), Walker begins a bend to Ab on beat 4 of measure 46, landing on the G (5th) in measure 47, and further carefully selects the 4th (F) and b7th (Bb) notes. Again, anticipating the next chord change, he bends the Ab on beat 4 of measure 47 to the "true blue note" between Ab (b3rd) and A (major 3rd) of F7 in measure 48. Before resolving to the tonic note of Bb in the turnaround in measures 49–50, Walker runs through the V (F7) chord in measure 48 with the root and b7th (Eb) notes.

Performance Tip: Observe the bend of the b7th (Eb) up to the root (F) on beats 2–3 in measure 48, which gives a short turbo-boost towards the turnaround.

Strollin' with Bones
    Example 3

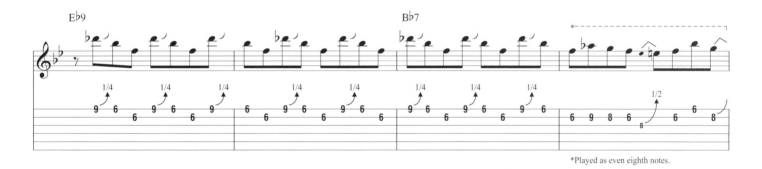

*Played as even eighth notes.

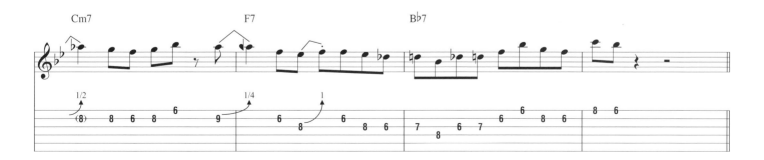

Section I

Letter I could easily be heard as the climactic section of the strutting tune as it boasts the most energy. It precedes the concluding six-measure Letter J, which features a truncated version of the signature horn riff (not shown) and ends with Walker arpeggiating B9 and Bb9 chords.

Hot on the heels of the four-measure octave horn riffs in measures 87–90 (not shown), Walker jumps in with another of his signature riffs: the thrillingly dissonant bent Bb diminished chord voicing over the I chord (Bb7) in measures 91–92. The result is not unlike a wailing siren.

In measures 93–94, descending, defining licks in the Bb composite blues scale over the I chord (Bb7) relax the taut musical tension. He includes a dynamic interval before up-shifting again in measure 95 with his famous bending unison lick, this time on the F note over the ii7 chord (Cm7). While it could be seen to function as the sus4 of C, it more likely anticipates the F7 in measure 96—a hip improvising trick B.B. King also employed.

Performance Tip: Check out how Walker repeats the F unison bend one more time on beat 1 of measure 96 as a form of resolution from the tension produced in measure 95. As is his wont, in measures 97–98, he tosses out one of his stock turnaround licks containing unmistakable resolution to the tonic chord.

Strollin' with Bones
Example 4

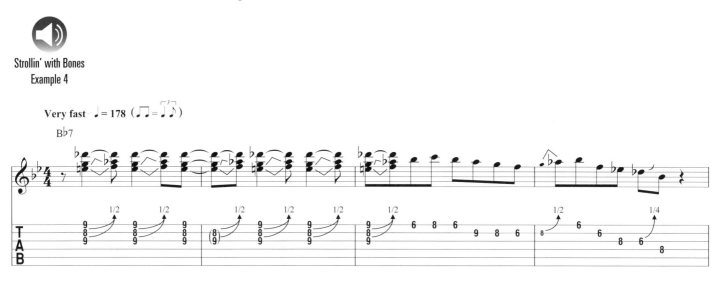

STROLLIN' WITH BONES

Words and Music by T-Bone Walker, Vida Lee Walker and Edward Davis, Jr.

Strollin' with Bones
Full Song

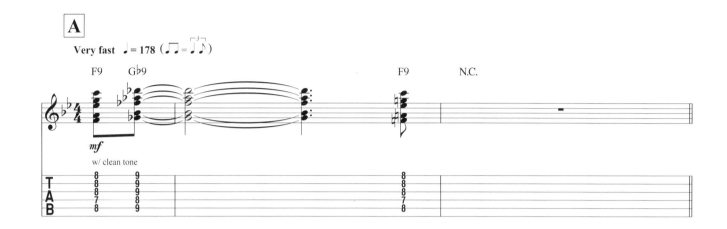

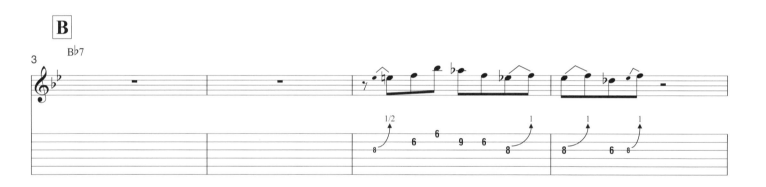

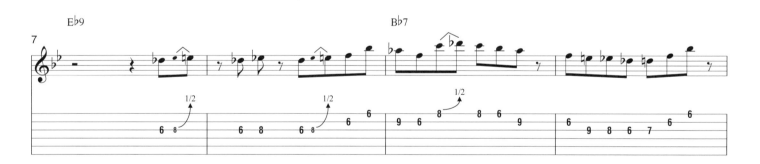

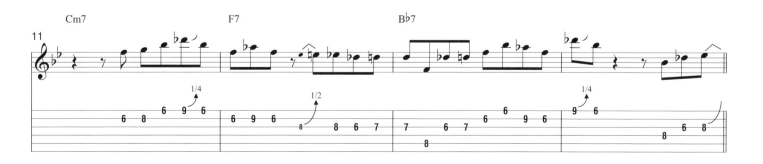

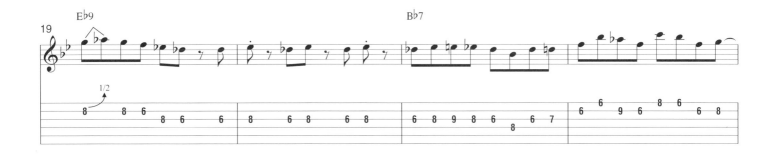

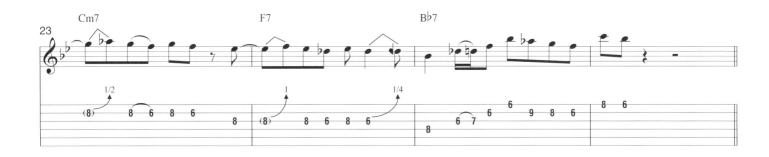

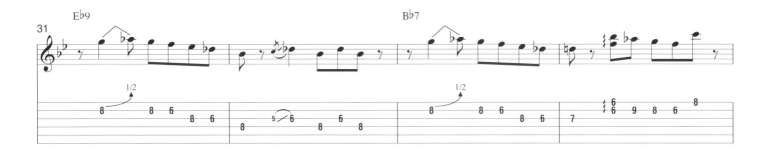

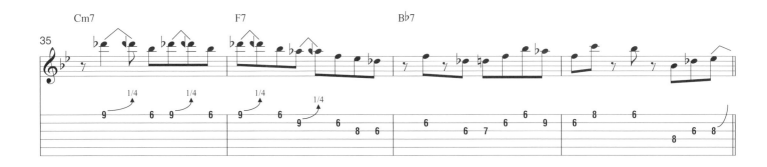

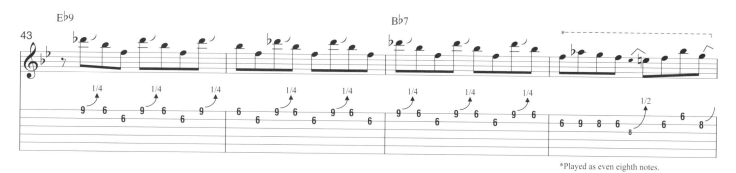

*Played as even eighth notes.

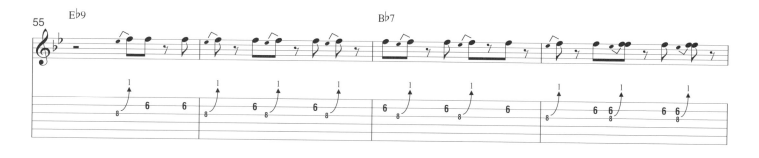

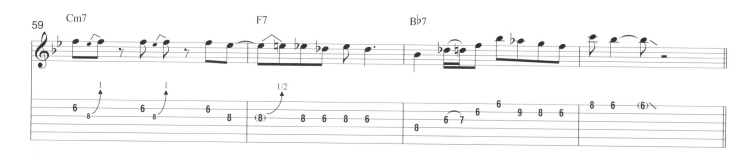

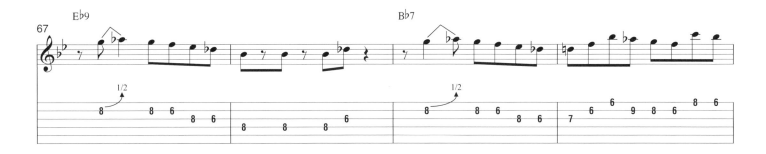

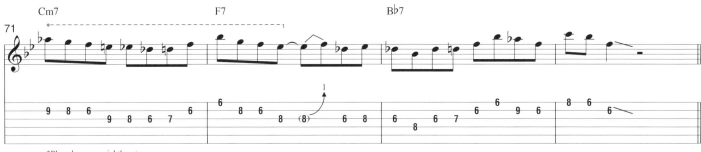

*Played as even eighth notes.

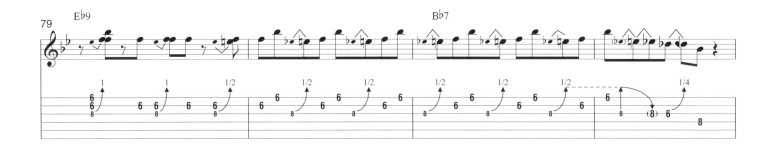

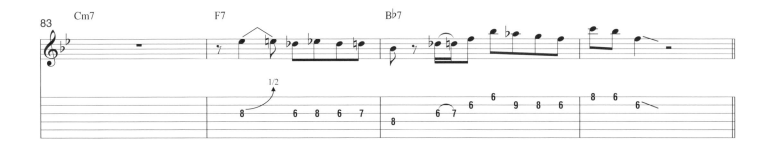

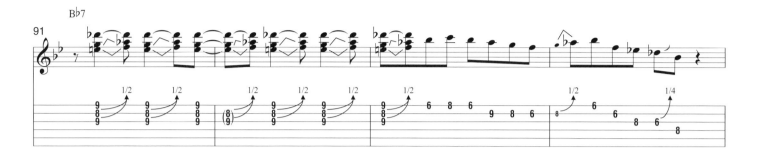

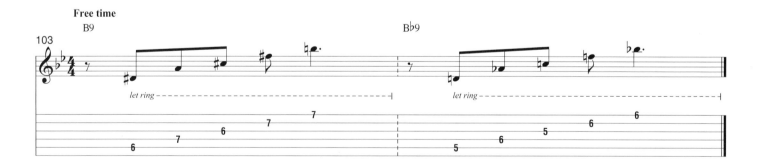

ESSENTIAL LICKS

Root-Position Composite Blues Scale

As shown previously in the Guitar Solo section of "Mean Old World," Walker spent virtually his entire career digging deep into the recesses of the root-position composite blues scale to reveal its timeless musical rewards. To say he "owned" it would not be an exaggeration. However, like literally every other blues guitarist, he had his favorite licks to use as improvisational "hacks" for his classic solos.

Lick 1

Walker always put his own spin on the "Blues 101" lick favored as an opener by many blues guitarists. Here he takes advantage of the A♭ composite blues scale to add the 6th (F) and 9th (B♭) notes as melodic interest on the way to the final destination of the ♭7th (G♭).

Performance Tip: Do not miss how the F note on beat 3 actually functions as the tonality-defining major 3rd of the IV chord (D♭7).

Lick 1

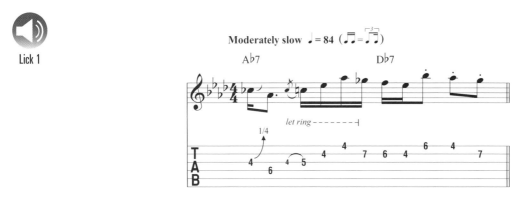

Lick 2

This valuable I chord (A♭9) lick comes in with tangy musical tension via the E♭ unison bends, and then resolves sweetly to the major 3rd (C) and 5th (E♭) to nail down the tonic harmony.

Performance Tip: Bend with the ring finger backed up by the middle finger.

Lick 2

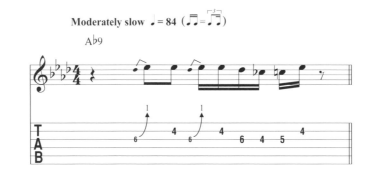

Lick 3

Walker was nowhere near a string-torturing bender like Albert King, for example. Nonetheless, he used indispensable blues guitar technique to great expressive effect through subtlety and nuance, as seen in this lick involving three different bent notes. Notice in particular the 4th (A♭) of the IV chord (E♭9) bent a quarter step, followed by the major 3rd (G) bent a half step to A♭ within beat 3.

Performance Tip: Bend the A♭ with the pinky and the G with the ring finger (see photo).

Lick 3

Lick 4

With utter simplicity, legato phrasing, and harmonic logic, Walker implies the I chord (Bb7) with the major 3rd (D) and root (Bb), and the V chord (F+7) with the root (F) in this turnaround lick.

Performance Tip: Observe the Db (augmented 5th of F+7) bent to D on beat 3 for a smidgen of tension preceding resolution to the root on beat 4.

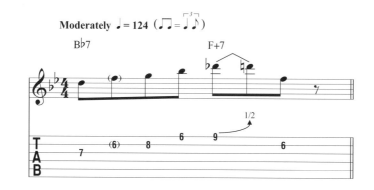

Lick 5

In this lick, Walker shows how to cut to the essence of a I chord change with a harmony-defining lick spanning two measures. He begins on the root and gracefully inches up the scale while executing rubbery, tension-inducing bends, before resolving back to where he began on the root (C). This lick could function as part of an improvised 12-bar blues chorus, or just as easily as a fill in a vocal verse.

Performance Tip: Bend the F notes on string 3 at fret 10 with the ring finger backed up by the middle and index fingers. Access the quarter-step bend on beat 3 in measure 2 by pulling *down* with the index finger.

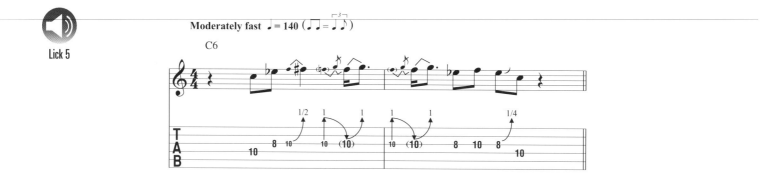

Lick 6

The fact that Walker often navigates chord changes more like a jazz guitarist than a blues guitarist of his era cannot be stressed enough. Over this IV chord (F9) lick, he still remains faithful to the root position of the C composite blues scale, but cunningly selects notes relative to F9. The descending chord tones of C (5th), G (9th), and F (root) in the first bar clue the listener in with certainty, while the repeated ♭7th notes (E♭) in the second bar complete the dominant tonality.

Performance Tip: Barre strings 1 and 2 with the index finger over beats 3 and 4 of the first bar and pick upward on strings 1 and 2, followed by a down stroke on string 3 for the ring finger bend on the F note.

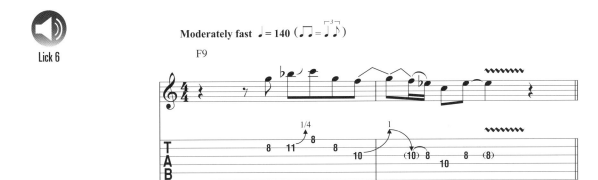

Lick 7

Though this lick would also convey appropriate musical information if played against the I chord (C6), it is hipper against the IV chord (F9) due to the C/G dyad functioning as the 5th/9th of that change.

Performance Tip: Barre C/G with the index finger. The F bent one half step under the G on beat 3 goes by quickly but is worth acknowledging for its quick hit of harmony.

Lick 8

Walker sounds way modern, like an aggressive post-war electric guitarist, in this lick that he recorded in 1944!
Over the I chord (C6) on beat 1, he bends the 4th (F) to the 5th (G) while simultaneously holding down the 6th (A)
to create the sumptuous harmony of A/G with the rhythm section. He defines the I chord (C6) with a more typical
dyad including the root and 5th (C and G) of the chord, before opting to throw a dash of pepper into the mix with the
quarter-step bend of the ♭3rd (E♭) to the "true blue note."

Performance Tip: Bend the F note with the ring finger while anchoring the A note with the pinky (see photo).

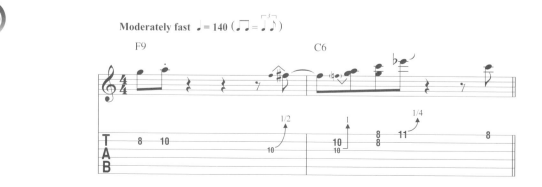

Lick 8

Lick 9

Smooth as the 20th Century Limited express passenger train in the 1940s, Walker deftly picks all 16th notes (including a 16th-note triplet) in the following lick—all in the service of complimenting the I chord (G7) tonality. Contributing to his seamless legato phrasing is his selection of composite blues scale notes, with the half steps adding melody beyond the basic blues scale.

Performance Tip: Check out the four notes on string 3 forming a compressed, chromatic line that reverses direction back to the root note.

Lick 9

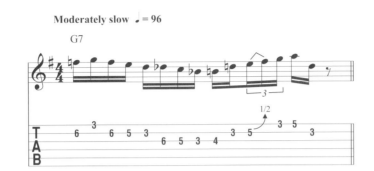

Lick 10

In this lick, Walker leaves no doubt as to the IV chord (C7) change with the inclusion of the root (C), 3rd (E), 5th (G), ♭7th (B♭), and 9th (D) of the chord.

Lick 10

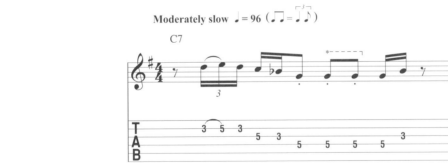

*Played as even eighth notes.

Lick 11

Never missing an opportunity to trot out his signature diminished triad, Walker employs it to stunning effect in this closing turnaround lick before resolving to a three-note G7 voicing.

Performance Tip: Low to high, use the middle, index, and ring fingers for the G diminished chord.

Lick 11

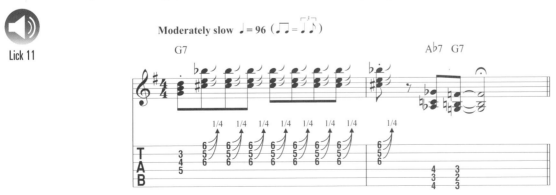

Lick 12

Walker injects a rich dollop of harmony into the welter of single-note lines found in this lick over the IV chord. He slides repeatedly into the Db/Bb (root/13th) dyad from a whole step below to enrich the IV chord (Db7) tonality.

Performance Tip: Access the dyad with the ring and index fingers, low to high.

Lick 12

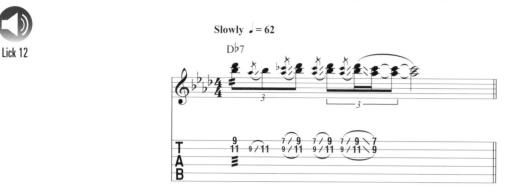

Lick 13

Walker follows the 5th (Eb) at fret 4 with the major 3rd (C) over the I chord (Ab) in an unusual manner by bending up from the b3rd (Cb), also at fret 4, resulting in a perceived time warp. He follows up with a hammer-on from the b3rd to the 3rd and rolls up the root position of the composite blues scale to extremely brief resolution on the root note (Ab). Rather than lingering, however, he continues with the b7th (Gb) and 5th (Eb) in 32nd and 16th notes, respectively, before closing on the 9th (Bb).

Performance Tip: Play the 5th with the index finger and bend the b3rd with the middle finger.

Lick 13

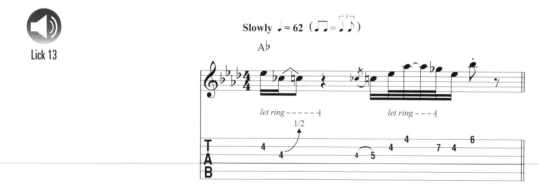

Lick 14

After resting for two beats over the I chord (Ab), Walker breaks out a snappy 16th-note lick containing a substantial interval between the one-step bend of the 4th (Db) to the 5th (Eb), followed quickly by the root (Ab). Running up the scale he nicks Cb (b3rd), Db, Eb, and Gb (b7th).

Performance Tip: Bend the Db with the ring finger backed up by the middle and index fingers. It will then take quick reflexes to drop the ring finger onto the root on string 4 in order to reset the hand to logically journey up the scale.

Lick 14

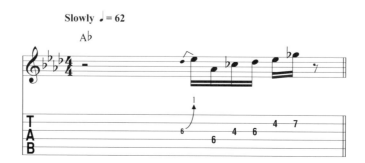

Lick 15

One of the earliest and greatest electric blues guitarists to cover both rhythm and lead equally and simultaneously, Walker had infallible intuition when accompanying himself. Sometimes it was as simple as playing a smooth combination like the lick seen here: a bass-string double stop, the 5th of the IV chord (Db9) on the low E string, a fat 9th chord (Db9), and a dyad "plucked" from the middle strings of the chord.

Performance Tip: Maintain the Db chord shape throughout the entire measure and fret the notes with the following fingers, low to high: middle, index, and ring finger (as a small barre on strings 3 and 2).

Lick 15

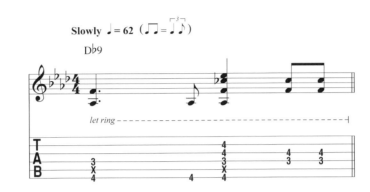

Lick 16

In the next lick, rather than bending to a unison note, Walker presents a variation on his signature bend by involving a 5th. He combines a one-step bend from the 4th (Db) to the 5th (Eb) of the I chord (Ab) and then plays the root (Ab) on string 1. Harkening back to country blues, it is more dynamic and dramatic. He also manages to fit in a quarter-step bend from the b3rd (Cb) to the "true blue note" on the "and" of beat 3. If that were not enough, he ends the measure of the I chord (Ab) by strumming a C7/G on the upbeat of beat 4 as a "grace chord" preceding the Db7/Ab in the following bar (not shown).

Performance Tip: Execute the one-step bends with the ring finger backed up by the middle and index fingers. Pull *down* on the b3rd with the index finger. Low to high, access the C7/G with the middle, index, and ring fingers.

Lick 16

Lick 17

Some licks are just perfect in light of their function as a tasty fill, yet can also be totally self-contained. Over the I–V (Ab–Eb7) chord change, Walker begins on the root and ends on the root. In between he bends the 4th (Db) of the I chord to the 5th (Eb), which becomes the root of the V chord (Eb7) across beats 2 and 3. On beat 4, he throws in a quarter-step bend on the b3rd (Cb, thinking now in relation to the I chord), but rather than resolving to the root, he jumps down to the 5th of the I chord on string 5 before resolving to the root on string 4 via the b7th (Gb).

Lick 17

Lick 18

Walker transitions from the I chord (A♭) to the V chord (E♭7) in this turnaround handsomely, and with little effort, as he arpeggiates the A♭ triad using 16th notes, ending succinctly on the root (E♭) of the V chord.

Performance Tip: Note the A9 chord on beat 4 serving as a "grace chord" leading to the A♭9 in the next measure (not shown).

Lick 18

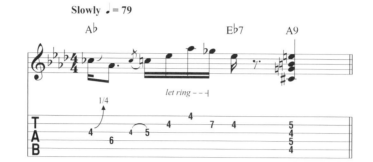

Lick 19

As should be apparent by now, Walker can pick bushels of 16th notes on command. However, he instinctively knows when to pull back and pace himself with steady eighth notes, as in a final slow blues turnaround. As expected, he acknowledges the root (A♭) of the I chord (A♭), followed by a slick walk down to the 5th (E♭) chromatically from the 6th (F) and ♯5th (F♭) notes. Somewhat surprisingly he ends on an E♭ instead of the tonic (A♭) on beat 1 of the final measure, where the harmony is the I chord (A♭). Sly cat that he is, he creates a touch of musical tension before resolving to A♭9 by preceding it with an A9 chord.

Lick 19

Lick 20

Following a sustained six-string IV chord (C9), Walker offers up yet another of his classic chordal riffs with implied 6th and 9th chords on beat 4.

Performance Tip: The C9 chord could be seen as C9/G as the 5th (G) is on the bottom. It should be fretted with the middle finger along with the C note as a small barre on strings 6 and 5 (see photo). **Performance Tip 2:** Play the sliding riff with the ring finger inasmuch as it is already on strings 3–1 via the C9 chord.

Lick 20

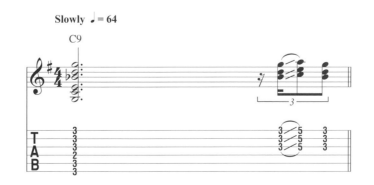

Lick 21

In this IV–I–IV progression, Walker plays a 6th/9th riff appropriate to the I chord (G7), in anticipation of its appearance in the second bar. He then repeats rhythmic variations before moving forward to more classic blues licks from the G composite blues scale.

Performance Tip: Play the sliding riff, low to high, with the middle, index, and ring fingers (see photo).

Lick 21

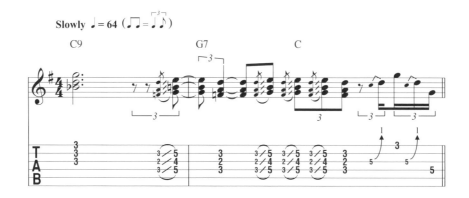

Lick 22

We find another elegantly simple blues lick complementing the IV chord (C9) with the ♭7th (B♭) and the root in this next lick. The quarter-step bend to the "true blue note" on the end of beat 4 creates a snippet of musical tension.

Performance Tip: Push up with the index finger for the B♭ quarter-step bend.

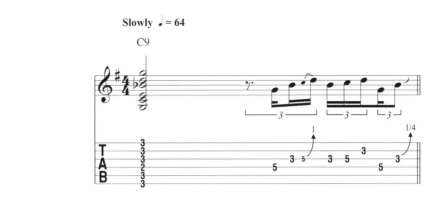

Lick 23

It can be startling to hear an early 1950s electric blues guitarist execute repeating unison bends on the 5th (D) of the I chord (G9) with such gusto. The texture creates tension and contrasts dynamically with the single-note lines that follow.

Performance Tip: For the unison bends, barre strings 2 and 1 with the index finger so that the root note (G) on string 1 may be accessed quickly and efficiently. Bend string 3 with the ring finger.

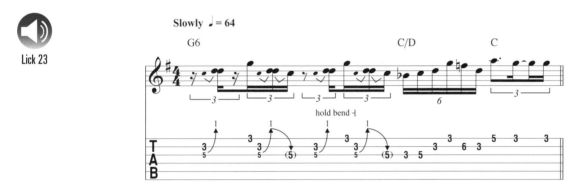

Lick 24

Another Walker signature accompaniment lick involves implying a 6th (or 13th) chord with bass-string notes (B♭) on beat 4, a half step above the ii7 chord (Am7) in the following measure (not shown).

Performance Tip: Use the middle finger for the B♭ and the index finger for the G.

SIGNATURE RIFFS

It is thought by some uninformed musicians that T-Bone Walker played the same solo over and over again. Though he had his passel of stock phrases like virtually all blues guitarists, it is patently not true. Subtlety and nuance, combined with a refined sense of melody and harmony, make every one of his solos an exceptionally expressive blues lesson worthy of inspection.

Bye Bye Baby (1953)
From *T-Bone Walker: The Ultimate Collection 1929–57* (Acrobat)

From the only session Walker recorded in Detroit with a territory band he knew well, the swinging shuffle shows him at the top of his game ten years on from his first significant recordings.

Intro

Walker foregoes his more typical single-string lead intro for unaccompanied comp chords instead. However, his decision serves a dual purpose as he demonstrates the tempo and rhythmic feel for the band.

The first seven measures consist of three two-chord phrases containing the V (F9) and #V (F#9) chords which resolve to the i chord (B♭m/F). As can be heard, "Texas-size" musical tension is created with this resolution to the minor chord, which could be seen as a curious choice, inasmuch as the tune is in the key of B♭ major. Relying on his knowledge of jazz, perhaps Walker surmised that the B♭m/F produces its own tension which fully resolves on the B♭7 chord appearing in measure 1 of Verse 1 (not shown).

Performance Tip: Due to the brisk tempo and propulsive rhythmic drive required, there is no room for error in the execution of the strums. In the F9 measures, strum up-up-down-up-down-up-up. In the F#9 measures, strum up-down-up-down-up-up. Strum down on the final F9 chord in measure 6. In measure 7, strum up-down-up-down-up for the B♭m/F chord. Be sure to mute the strings completely after each chord sequence by releasing the tension with the left hand, without removing the fingers from the strings, and by simultaneously coming down with the heel of the right hand near or on the bridge.

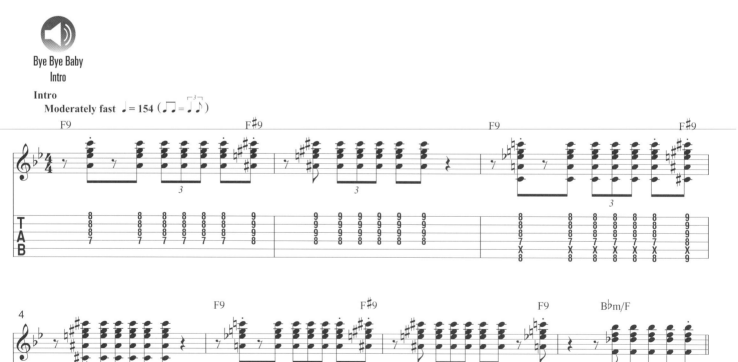

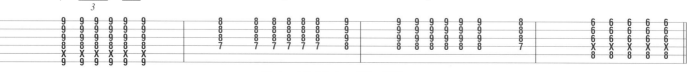

Guitar Solo

The two choruses of 12-bar blues comprising the guitar solo could suffice as a concise, yet inclusive sampling of Walker's improvisational wares. Besides his ever-vigilant acknowledgement of the chord changes, there are his cool signature riffs. Measure 1 contains a tantalizing taste of a repeating three-note riff featuring the "true blue note" between the ♭3rd (D♭) and major 3rd (D) of the I chord (B♭7).

Performance Tip: Bend the D♭ with the pinky followed by the index as a small barre at fret 6 for the B♭ on string 1 and the F on string 2.

Measures 2 and 3 highlight the famous unison bend on the 5th (F). The beauty of the sequential chords (part of the circle of 4ths) is the way the F creates tension as a sus4 over the ii chord (Cm) in measure 2, while in measure 3, it functions as the root of the V chord (F7).

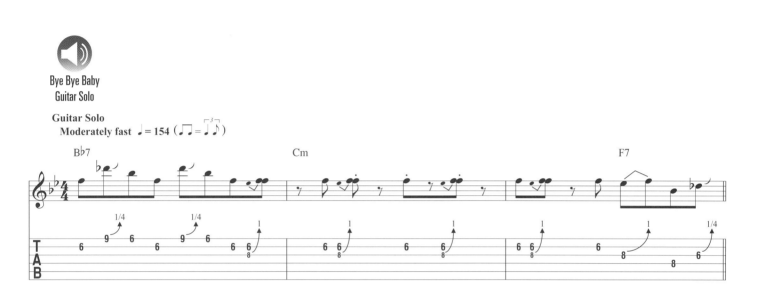

Bye Bye Baby
Guitar Solo

Don't Leave Me Baby (1946)
From *T-Bone Walker: The Ultimate Collection 1929–57*

From one of his many landmark post-war Hollywood sessions, this version prominently features Joe "Red" Kelly (trumpet) and Jack McVea (tenor sax) riffing away in the jumping horn section (also notated here for reference).

Intro

Even a cursory listen to Walker's guitar style reveals the influence of the horn section. In the four-measure Intro (with pick up notes), he honks mostly on the 5th (F) like a tenor sax man.

Performance Tip: Observe the chromatic line of F–F♯–G–G♯–A in measure 4 leading to the tonic note (B♭) in measure 1 of Guitar Solo 1 (not shown). The boost in forward motion is like flooring a flathead V-8 Ford.

Don't Leave Me Baby
Intro

Guitar Solo 2

Again, taking his seat in the horn section, Walker strums down with authority on the I chord (B♭) in combination with the horns in the first four measures of each 12-bar chorus in his 24-measure solo. In the next three measures of the first blues chorus, he decides to keep the pot on boil by resorting to his favorite unison bend off the 5th (F).

Check out measures 9–10, where he deliberately jumps in on the 3rd (A) of the V chord (F9) by bending the G one step in measure 9, and then hones in on the root (F) in measure 10. His effective, if typical, turnaround—resolving early to the I chord (B♭)—perfectly sets up the bleating horn blasts that follow.

The final eight measures of the solo demonstrate what may be admired over and over again in Walker's music, as he churns out swinging eighth-note lines as naturally and effortlessly as most people speak. Contributing to the effect is his reliance on the half steps in the B♭ composite blues scale, as seen in measure 20 over the I chord (B♭13) and in measure 21 over the V chord (F9). In addition, by playing the G (13th) and C (9th) of the altered I chord (B♭13) in the penultimate measure, Walker emphasizes the dominant quality of the chord.

Performance Tip: Most guitarists will find it easiest to play the B♭ chords in the solo by barring across the top two or three strings at fret 6 with the index finger and holding down the D on string 3 at fret 7 with the middle finger. Play the root on string 4 at fret 8 with the ring finger.

Don't Leave Me Baby
Guitar Solo 2

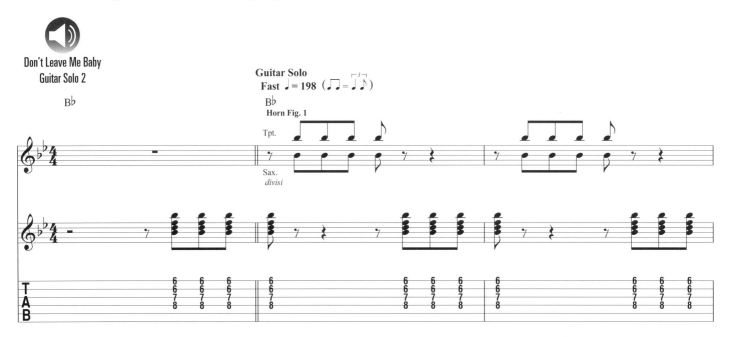

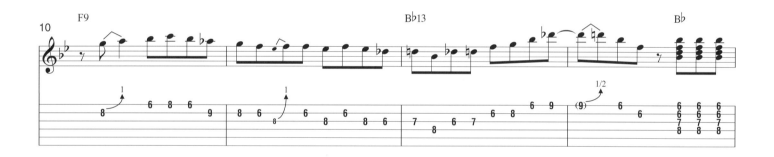

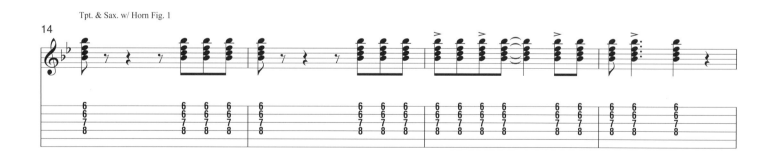

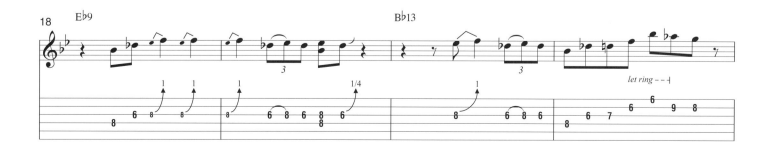

Ending

Filling the available musical space with vibrant harmony until the very end, Walker cashes out over the closing measures with a tangy bent B♭7 voicing (sans the root) on the top three strings. The extra two measures tagged on allow for extra long sustain of the B♭9 chord.

Performance Tip: As usual, finger the B♭7 chord bends as if they were a first-position D7. The four-note B9 and B♭9 chords are played, low to high, with the index, ring, middle, and pinky fingers.

Don't Leave Me Baby
Ending

Hard Pain Blues (1946)
From *T-Bone Walker: The Ultimate Collection 1929–57*

Waxed at the same Hollywood session producing the classics "I'm in an Awful Mood" and "It's a Low Down Dirty Deal," listening to this exquisite recorded performance will take away the "hard pain blues."

Intro/Guitar Solo 1

The four-measure Intro and eight-measure Guitar Solo combine for 12 bars of "slow change" in an arrangement unique to Walker, and indeed the blues in general. Though the four measures of the Intro essentially could be seen to function as the space for the I chord (B♭), they are arranged as repeating measures of ♯V chord (G♭9) to V chord (F9) strums. The resulting musical tension and anticipation are briefly resolved in measure 4 by moving from the ♭II chord (C♭9) to the I chord (B♭9).

The first two measures of Guitar Solo 1 contain the IV chord (E♭9), as the progression advances logically to complete the chorus of slow 12-bar blues. Also contributing to the distinctiveness of the arrangement is the I (B♭9)–vi (Gm7)–ii (Cm7)–V (F7) chord change in measures 8–9. Never missing a chance to delve deeper into basic I–IV–V blues progressions, Walker makes sure to repeat B♭ notes over the Gm7 where they function as the crucial ♭3rd.

Performance Tip: Listen to the track after carefully perusing the Intro. The suggested strumming direction for the G♭9 chord in bars 2 and 3 is down-up-down-up-down, followed by a down strum on the F9.

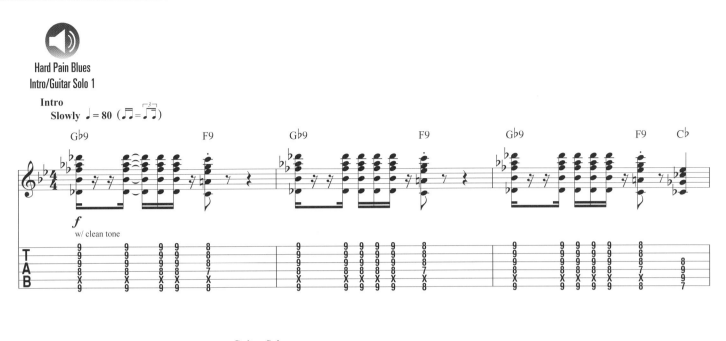

Hard Pain Blues
Intro/Guitar Solo 1

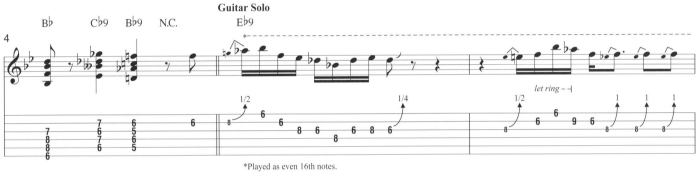

*Played as even 16th notes.

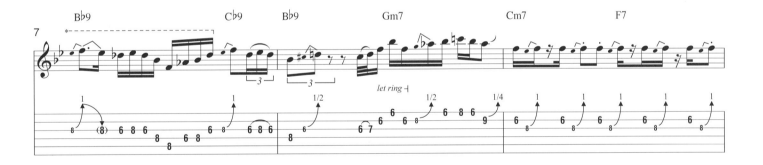

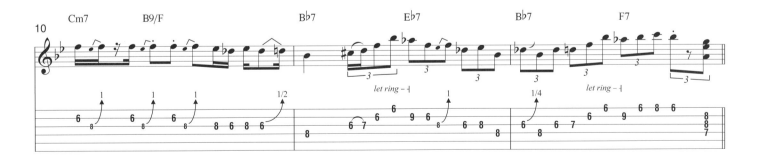

Guitar Solo 2

Like the vocal verses (not shown), the second Guitar Solo contains the "fast change." Besides his always liquid phrasing and satiny tone, Walker inserts several measures of sweet dyads in 3rds to contrast with the skeins of single notes. Over the IV chord (Eb9) in measures 5 and 6, he slides repeatedly on strings 1 and 2, moving up one step from Db/Bb (b7th/5th) to Eb/C (root/6th). The sustained Db/Bb dyad over beats 3 and 4 of measure 5 serves to enhance the dominant quality of the chord change.

Not satisfied with creating that sumptuous aural treat, Walker decides to continue the harmonic concept into the I chord (Bb9), anticipating the chord change by switching to strings 3 and 2 and sliding Ab/F (4th/9th) to Bb/G (5th/3rd) on beat 4 of measure 6. In measures 7 and 8, Ab/F functions as the b7th/5th of the I chord (Bb9).

Performance Tip: Play the 3rds on strings 2 and 1 with the ring and index fingers, respectively. Play the 3rds on strings 3 and 2 with the middle and index fingers, respectively.

Hard Pain Blues
Guitar Solo 2

*Played as even 16th notes.

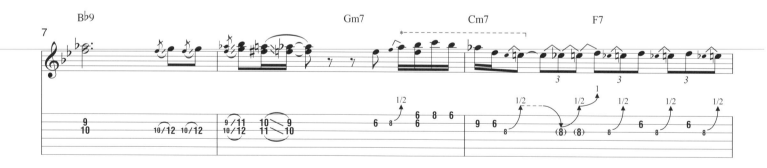

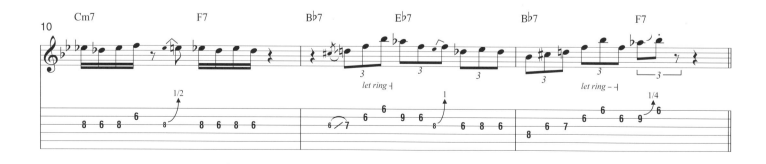

I Know Your Wig Is Gone (1947)
From *T-Bone Walker: The Ultimate Collection 1929–57*

Walker shows his affinity for and knowledge of jazz with a skillful arrangement of 16- and eight-measure sections. The legendary blues pianist Lloyd Glenn accompanies unobtrusively.

Intro

The eight-measure Intro is similar to the Outro (not shown) and introduces a selection of the chord voicings employed throughout. Most of the sections are constructed from four-measure chord progressions which begin with the I chord (B♭) and end on the V (F7) chord. Walker plays the lilting "head" derived from the B♭ composite blues scale alongside John "Teddy" Buckner (trumpet) and Hubert "Bumps" Myers (tenor sax).

Performance Tip: Observe the way the first two-measure phrase ends on the ♭♭7th (D♭) of the E°7 chord for anticipation, and the second two-measure phrase ends on the root of the V chord (F7) for resolution.

I Know Your Wig Is Gone
Intro

Guitar Solo 1

One of his typical improvised solos, Walker fashions a four-measure melodic pattern which could have served as a cool bluesy motif if repeated. It is based around the ♭7th (A♭) of the I chord (B♭) bent one half step to the major 7th (A), followed by the tonic (B♭) and the dyad of B♭/F (root/5th).

Performance Tip: Perform the bends in the last two measures with the pinky backed up by the ring, middle, and index fingers.

I Know Your Wig Is Gone
Guitar Solo 1

Guitar Solo 2

Combining just two four-measure ideas, Walker creates a jaunty eight-measure solo preceding the Bridge and last Verse (not shown). Similar to Guitar Solo 1, he employs double stops to significant dynamic effect. The tangy B/F♯ chromatic neighboring tones in the second measure of the solo add spice to the turnaround.

Performance Tip: Be aware that the notes B and F♯ do not appear in the B♭ composite blues scale, as Walker ventures "outside" and gives a wink and a nod to bebop jazz! **Performance Tip 2:** The B9 and B♭9 at the end of the example are actually first-inversion voicings (due to the 3rd on the bottom); they have become synonymous with the rhythm guitar style of Walker.

I Know Your Wig Is Gone
Guitar Solo 2

Glamour Girl (1950)
From *T-Bone Walker: The Ultimate Collection 1929–57*

Tenor and baritone sax player Big Jim Wynn formed a band with fellow Texan Walker in the mid-1930s. Starting in the late-1940s, Wynn became a sideman for his old friend and appears on this track with tenor sax giant Eddie "Lockjaw" Davis. Also included is lauded blues drummer Robert "Snake" Sims, who backed Walker for 15 years. Like the guitarist, Wynn was a showman and one of the first tenor honkers to jump up and roll around on the stage floor while soloing.

Unusual in the T-Bone Walker canon, there is no guitar solo in "Glamour Girl."

Verse 1

In what might be an historically early example of the lick, Walker executes a slinky, double-string bend and release from F/D♭ to G♭/E♭ on strings 2 and 3 in measure 4. It is open to speculation as to whether or not the lap steel guitar-like sound was influenced by Eddie Durham, who recorded the first electric blues solo with an amplified lap steel guitar in 1935 on "Hittin' the Bottle."

Performance Tip: Though open to personal choice, try accessing the double-string bend with the ring and pinky fingers, low to high (see photo).

Even more significant are the jazzy chord substitutions over the I chord (A♭) in measures 4–6. An ascending chord sequence of A♭ (I), B♭m (ii), Bm (♭iii), Cm (iii), and D♭6 (IV) leads dramatically to E♭m (v). Not finished with his chord cornucopia however, on beat 4 of measure 5, Walker drops back a half step to a D9 (♭V) resolving to D♭9 (IV).

Also of importance, in measures 8–9, Walker's embellishment of the harmony with moving dyads on strings 5 and 4 include the 3rds and ♭7ths from his signature first-inversion 9th chord voicing. It is arguably his most famous signature rhythm guitar technique, as the implied moving chord voicings contribute considerable harmonic weight to his blues progressions. Walker neatly wraps up the sequence by connecting the root note of A♭7 on string 1 to a triplet with the implied A♭9 voicing on beat 3 of measure 9. Forging ahead gracefully and logically, he follows on beat 4 with the 5th (C♭) and 3rd (A♭) of F♭7 (or E7) which leads smartly to the V chord (E♭7) in measure 10.

Performance Tip: Access the dyads with the index and ring fingers, low to high. This will place the left hand in an advantageous position to reach the two A♭ notes on string 1 with the pinky finger while leaving the middle finger free to play the C♭ notes on string 6.

Glamour Girl
Verse 1

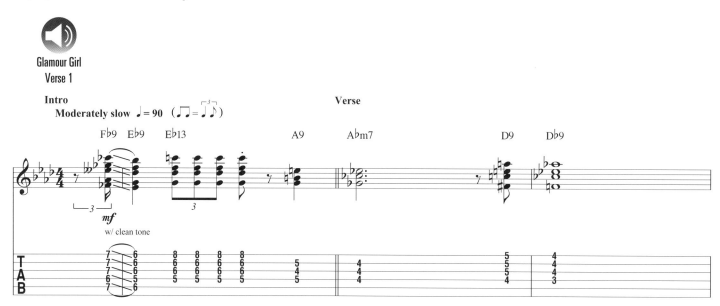

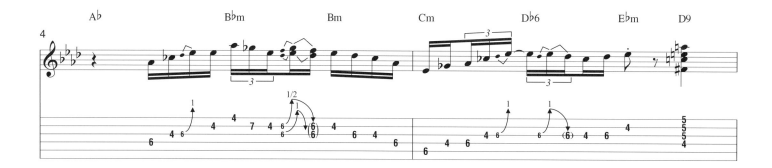

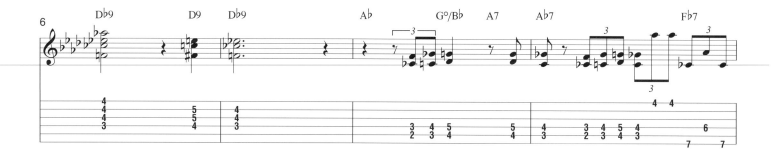

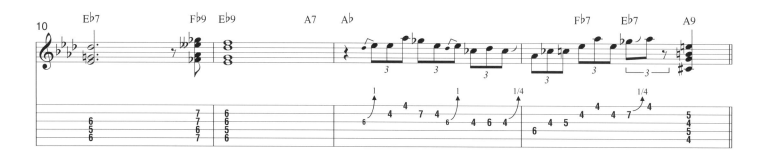

Verse 2

Related to the moving dyads in Verse 1, in Verse 2, Walker utilizes his full four-note, first-inversion 9th voicings to produce an outstanding string of rich harmony featuring dynamic leaps in register. Be aware that the final chord of this section (A9) descends by one half step to resolve on the I chord (A♭9) in Verse 3 (not shown). The A9 functions as a substitution for the V chord (E♭9) on the previous beat.

**Glamour Girl
Verse 2**

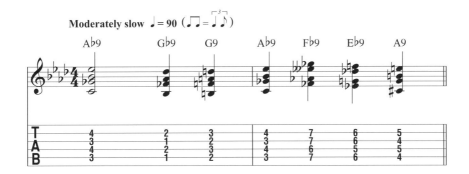

Verse 4

Completing his "T-Bone 101" course on 9th chords, Walker "deserts" his "Glamour Girl" in the final two measures of the song with a dramatic, ascending, chromatic series of 9th chords connecting the IV chord (D9) to the I chord (A♭9).

Performance Tip: Use the following fingering for the 9th chords, low to high: middle finger, index finger, and ring finger as a barre on strings 3 and 2.

**Glamour Girl
Verse 4**

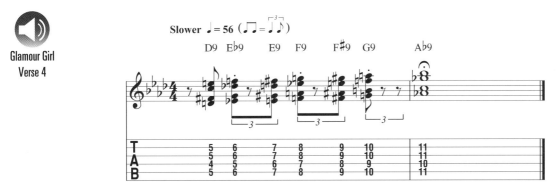

You Don't Love Me (1950)
From *T-Bone Walker: The Ultimate Collection 1929–57*

From the same galvanic session as "Glamour Girl," Walker flaunts his virtuosity while forging the benchmark for blues-jazz guitarists with a textbook of slick licks and riffs. Contributing to his stunning artistry is the prominent presence of the "out-of-phase" tone of his 1949 Gibson ES-5.

Intro

Walker stretches out considerably in the two-chorus, 24-measure Intro. Measures 1–4, including the pick up, are essentially unaccompanied "call and response" with the horn section. Observe how he ends the lick connecting the pick-up measure with measure 1 on G, the 5th scale degree of C7. The second lick connecting measures 1 and 2 ends on C, the 5th scale degree of F7.

Performance Tip: Though the 5th of a chord does not create as much anticipation or implied forward motion as the ♭7th, it does not create resolution either. Therefore, it can be a good option when desiring to keep a section bopping along.

The unaccompanied measures illustrate the way common notes from the root position of the blues scale can be turned into a most memorable phrase through the "prestidigitation" produced by a "wave" of Walker's "magic" right hand. In other words, after the appropriate note selection, it is all in the phrasing.

You Don't Love Me
Intro Part 1

Intro
Moderately ♩ = 100

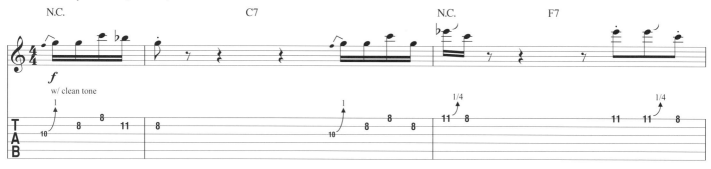

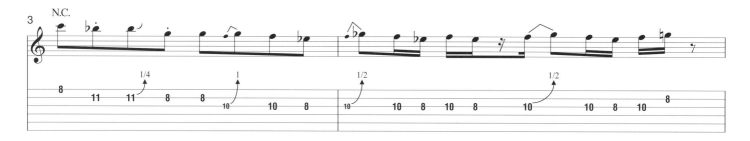

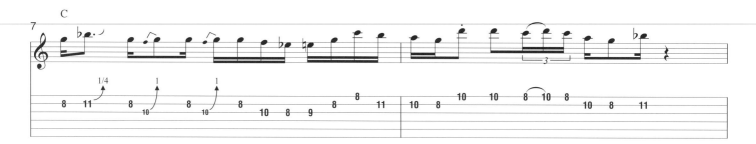

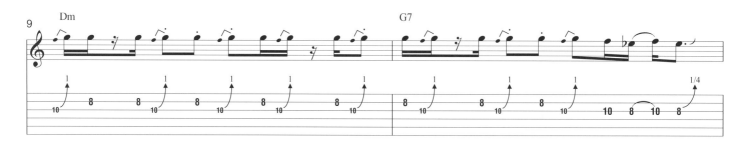

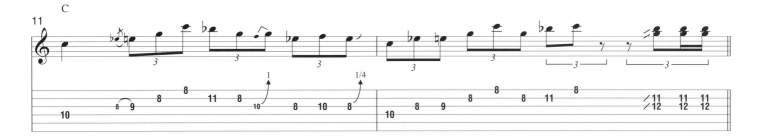

The second chorus of 12-bar blues comes in like a locomotive bearing down on Los Angeles from Texas. In the first three measures, churning dyads of Bb/G (b7th/5th) build a "head of steam" through repeating 16th-note sextuplets over the I chord (C). In the next measure, Walker produces yet more musical anticipation by moving between C7–C#7–C7; the anticipation is made even more dynamic by the rests that follow.

Classic, undulating "T-Bone licks" grace measures 5–8, while over the ii chord (Dm) in measure 9, he employs an unusual descending run of triplets, surprisingly involving open strings as the third note of each one.

Performance Tip: Check out how the last open string in measure 9 is G, anticipating the V chord (G7) in measure 10.

You Don't Love Me
Intro Part 2

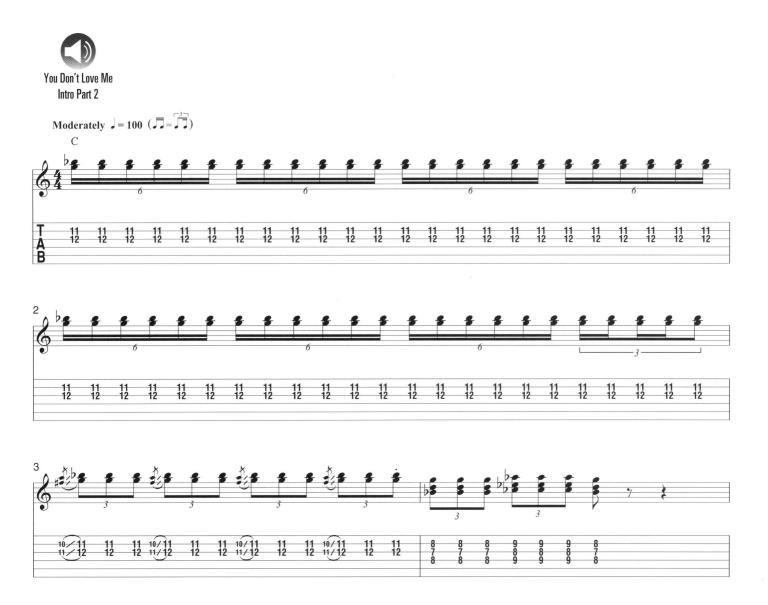

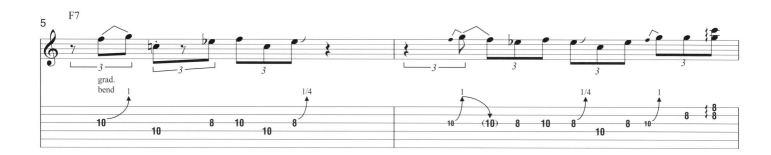

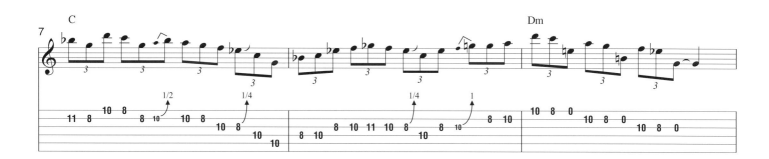

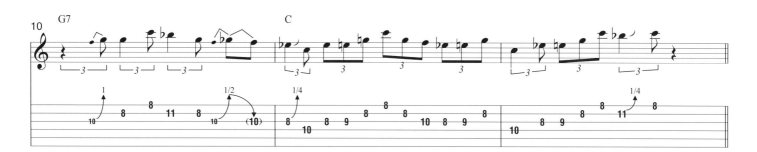

Verse 3

Perhaps more than any other blues guitarist of the era—with Johnny Moore a close second—Walker was nearly as expressive with chords as he was with single-note runs. The closing two measures of the song feature sophisticated jazz voicings in sync with the horn section, travelling from C7#9 (I) to C13 (I) in the hippest of harmonic arrangements!

Performance Tip: Finger as follows (low to high, with repeated fingers indicating a barre): C7#9 = pinky, middle, index, index; Cadd2 = pinky, middle, index, index; Db = ring, middle, index, index; Bb9 = index, ring, ring, ring; G7 = index, middle, index, index; Db9 =index, ring, ring, ring. C13 = index, ring, ring, pinky.

You Don't Love Me
Verse 3

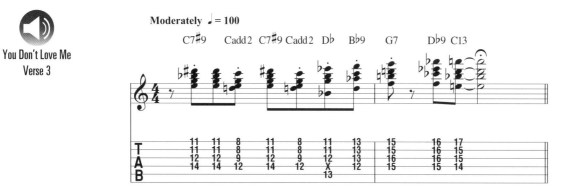

No Worry Blues (1947)
From *T-Bone Walker: The Ultimate Collection 1929–57*

A blues tune where the singer has "no worries" about his "baby" is rare in the history of the genre. Though not transcribed, the obligattos of tenor saxophonist Jack McVea and trumpeter Joe "Red" Kelly are well worth hearing, as they weave in and out with Walker in the verses.

Intro/Guitar Solo

One of the many signature intros Walker was fond of combined steady "mandolin strumming" on the V and ♯V chords, resolving to the V7, immediately followed by an arpeggiated V+ (augmented chord) to create anticipation. He uses this type of intro in "No Worry Blues," and with brilliant musical vision, he ties it right into a lick from the A♭ composite blues scale in measure 2, which flows like honey on a summer day into the I chord (A♭7) in the first bar of the Guitar Solo.

Performance Tip: For the E♭+ chord, access the strings (low to high) with the ring, middle, and then the index finger as a small barre on strings 3 and 2.

In measures 7–9, Walker inserts sweet harmony into the middle of his solo via dyads containing D♭/B♭ (root/6th) for the IV chord (D♭7), and A♭/F (root/6th) for the I chord (A♭7).

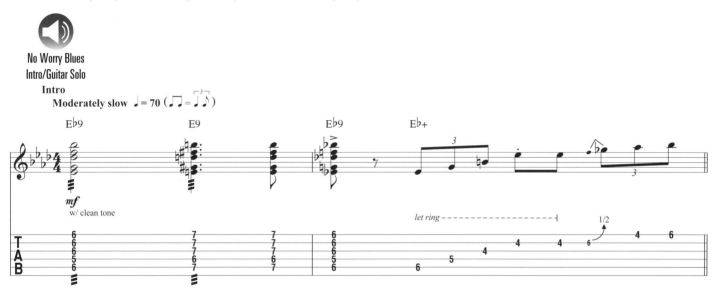

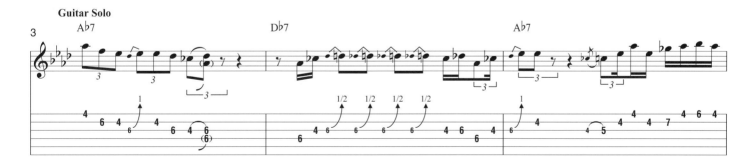

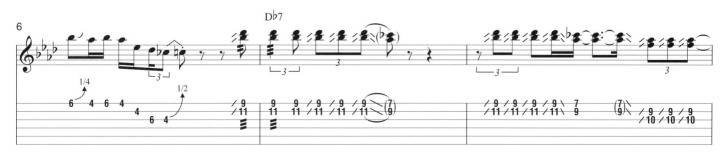

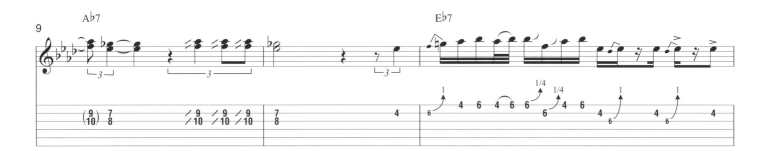

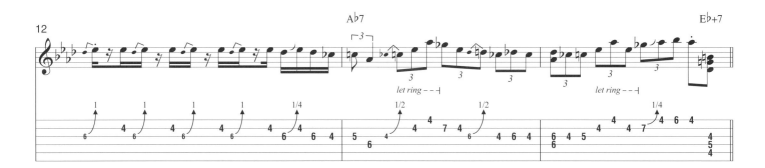

Verse 2

Like his contemporary Johnny Moore (who backed Charles Brown in the 1940s), Walker relied heavily on two main 9th-chord voicings. For the I chord (A♭9), he mostly went with the "T-Bone voicing" of a first-inversion 9th chord on the middle four strings. For the IV chord (D♭9), he utilizes a classic four-string version of the 9th chord with the root on string 5; the point being to keep both voicings on the middle four strings for efficiency of fingering and consistency of register.

Performance Tip: Displaying his keen ear for rhythmic expression, Walker slides with a syncopated snap into the I chord (A♭9) from one fret above in measures 3, 4, 7, and 8.

In measure 11, Walker lets loose with his stunning bent diminished 7th chord on strings 4–1. The result is a siren-like alarm signaling the impending end of the song in measure 12.

Performance Tip: Low to high, finger the diminished chord with the index, ring, middle, and pinky. Observe how the fingering of the diminished chord on strings 4–1 is exactly like the first-inversion 9th chord on strings 5–2. Bend the chord a quarter step by pushing up slightly on all four strings simultaneously.

No Worry Blues
Verse 2

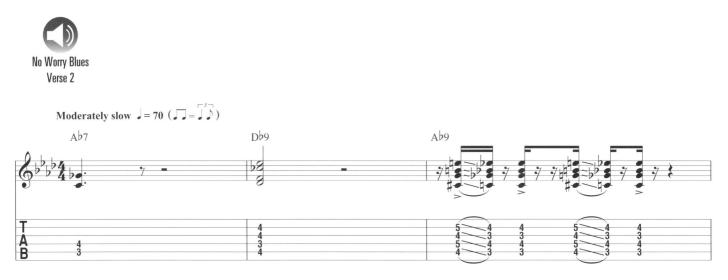

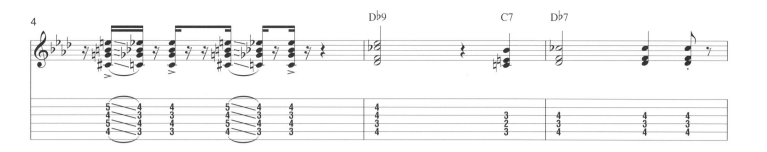

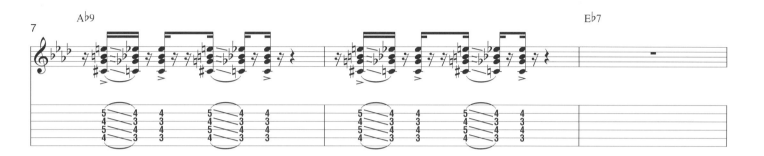

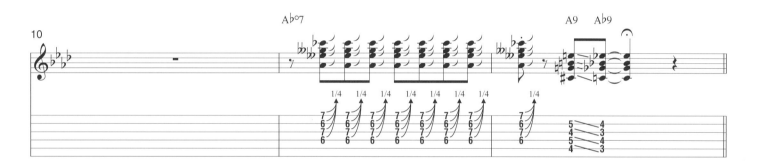

She Had to Let Me Down (1947)
From *T-Bone Walker: The Ultimate Collection 1929–57*

This song was recorded on the same landmark day in Hollywood as "(They Call It) Stormy Monday," "I Know Your Wig Is Gone," and "T-Bone Jumps Again," featuring the legendary blues pianist Lloyd Glenn.

Intro

Arguably, this is the most sophisticated slow blues chord intro in the Walker canon, with lush harmony worth analyzing. The four measures consist of two two-measure descending cadences moving from the I chord (Ab9) to the V chord (Eb9). In measures 1 and 2, the progression descends through the bVII chord (Gb9), #V chord (E7), and V chord (Eb9). However, note how Walker embellishes the changes in measures 3 and 4 by slipping 13th chords in between the voicings to gently accelerate the forward momentum.

Performance Tip: The 9th chords are typically played, low to high, with the middle, index, and the ring finger as a barre on strings 3–1. Converting them to 13th chords is easily accomplished by barring strings 2–1 with the pinky, two frets above the ring finger barre.

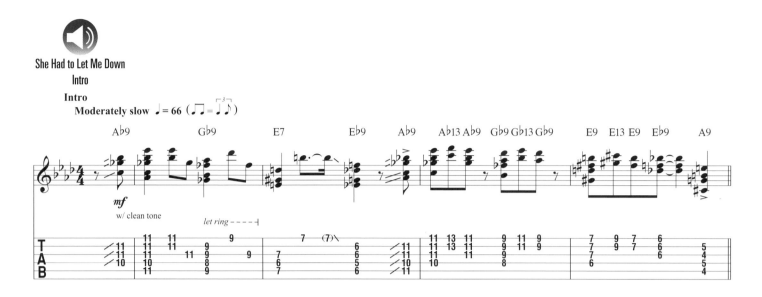

She Had to Let Me Down
Intro

Verse 2

At the end of Verse 2, Walker figuratively dances over the strings in nimble 16th notes derived from the A♭ composite blues scale. Contributing to the uninterrupted, sinuous flow of lyricism is the half-step movement between the 6th (F) and ♭7th (G♭) notes, and also between the ♭3rd (C♭), 3rd (C), and 4th (D♭) notes.

Performance Tip: Audio and visual evidence seems to confirm Walker used virtually all down strokes, even in sprightly single-note passages. That said, some combination of alternate picking is recommended for us mere mortals!

She Had to Let Me Down
Verse 2

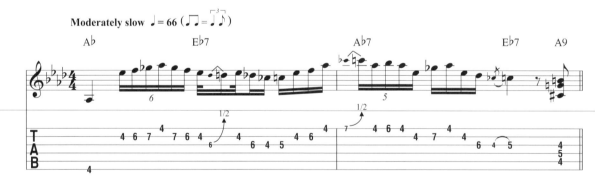

Verse 3

Flaunting hip chordal chops in Verse 3, Walker shows the value of knowing various voicings related to a chord when filling between vocal lines. Observe how he combines a rootless A♭°7 triple stop, a dyad on the 4th fret implying an A♭ major chord, and a triple stop signifying A♭6/9.

Performance Tip: For the A♭°7 triple stop, use the middle, index, and ring fingers, low to high; bend the strings by pushing up slightly with all three fingers simultaneously. For the A♭/E♭ dyad at fret 4, barre with the index finger. Barre with the ring finger for the A♭6/9 at fret 6.

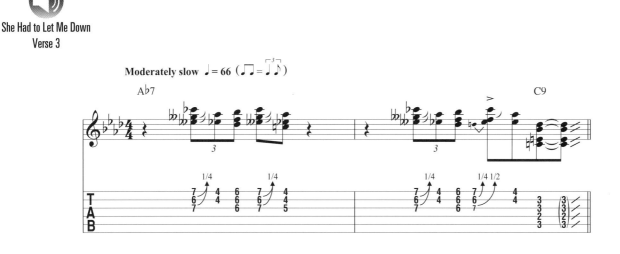

She Had to Let Me Down
Verse 3

T-Bone Boogie (1945)
From *T-Bone Walker: The Ultimate Collection 1929–57*

"T-Bone Boogie" was recorded at a session in Chicago with pianist/arranger Marl Young. Young would move to Los Angeles and become instrumental in merging the all-black and all-white musician's unions there in 1953. In addition, he was the first black director of a major network TV show in the early 1970s (for *Here's Lucy* starring Lucille Ball).

Intro

In measures 1–4, Walker shows how he can also employ the most minimal of means to crank up his 1945 model "V-8." After picking a string of root notes (C) without accompaniment in measure 1, he ends the phrase on the 5th (G) of the I chord (C) in measure 2, encouraging anticipation for the next measure. After repeating the swinging C notes in measure 3, he resolves to the root (C) in measure 4; this precedes the "Charleston rhythm" horn part, which is employed to finish out the first 12 measures of the Intro.

T-Bone Boogie
Intro Part 1

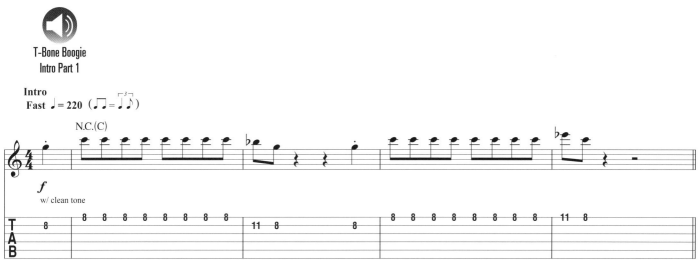

Walker then revs up the second 12-bar progression of the Intro with his iconic repeating "5th lick" unaccompanied, over an implied I chord (C). The last bar contains a short run resolving on the root (C).

Performance Tip: Walker slides into the 5th (G) on string 3, rather than bending up to it from the 4th (F). Be aware how this approach is similar to the way Charlie Christian executed the same lick.

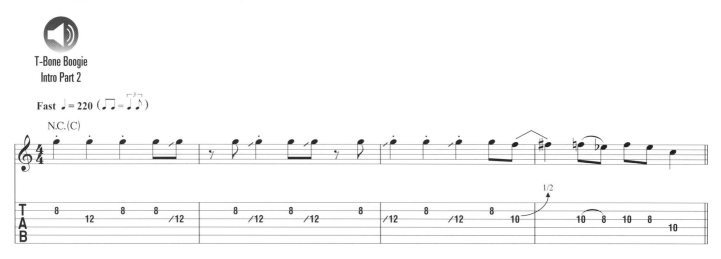

Guitar Solo

Walker romps and rolls through four 12-bar blues choruses like an unimpeded Texas tumbleweed. Throughout, he flashes his mastery of many blues guitar techniques, including rhythmic variation. For example, in the first chorus, he resorts to quarter-note triplets, instead of his typical swung eighths, to "make time stand still."

Performance Tip: Try all steady down strokes to keep from slipping into swung eighths time.

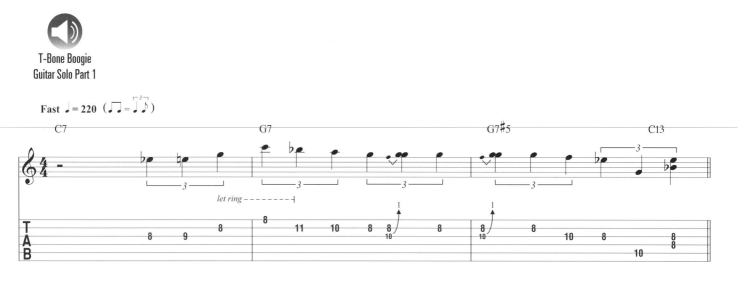

In measures 1–7 of the second 12-bar chorus, Walker hangs onto the bend of the 6th (A) of the I chord (C7) on string 2 for a beat and a half, followed by the root (C) as a quick eighth note to again "mess with the time." The result produces a perceived "slowing down" of time, adding yet more variety to the fast swing rhythm of the song.

T-Bone Boogie
Guitar Solo Part 2

The third and fourth choruses feature a repeating, clanging Walker chordal riff, big and bold enough to stand up in "call and response" with the bleating horn section. Consisting of a C°7 triad bent a half step to a C7 triple stop, it pumps the end of the tune to a rousing close—unusual in its intensity even for him.

Performance Tip: Play the diminished triad with the middle, index, and ring fingers, low to high. It is an efficient fingering because it allows the hand to easily access frets 8 and 10 with the index finger as a small barre. Note that Walker also utilizes the barre form to function as a "quick F6" in measures 5 and 17. Likewise, the barre functions as a ii chord (Dm) substitute for the I chord (C7) in measures 7, 9, 13, 15, and 19. He gets even more mileage out of the form in measure 22 as an implied G9 chord.

T-Bone Boogie
Guitar Solo Part 3

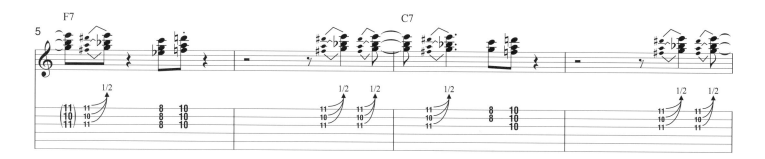

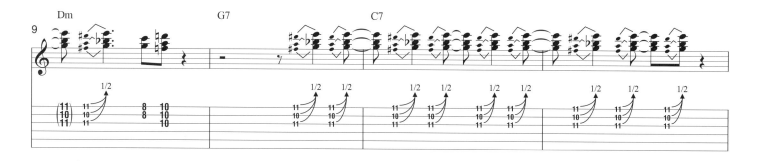

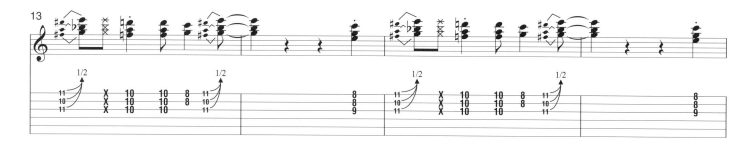

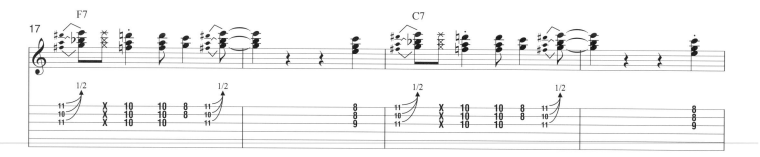

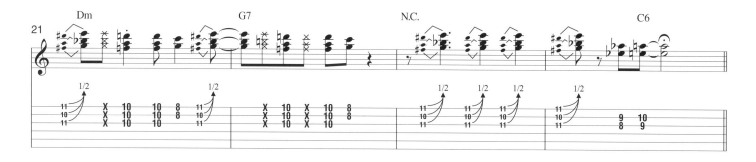

T-Bone Jumps Again (1947)
From *T-Bone Walker: The Ultimate Collection 1929–57*

Waxed at the same session as "(They Call It) Stormy Monday," "T-Bone Jumps Again" is one of Walker's classic instrumentals. Though the title likely refers to the style of up-tempo, swinging blues shuffles that came to be known as "jump blues," it also could be seen as a reference to his days as a dancer, and his show-stopping trick of jumping down into the splits while playing the guitar behind his head.

Section A

Walker joins the horn section for the "head" in measures 1–4 of the eight-measure section. Playing along with the melody (with the addition of dyads in 4ths), he blends in to produce a rich, sonorous sound, while standing out just enough to make his presence known.

Performance Tip: The four measures contain two two-measure riffs, differing only in the length of time the B/F♯ (7th/♯4) dyad is held down. It is tantalizingly sustained for two beats in measures 1 and 3, and then only for one beat in measures 2 and 4.

Walker transitions smoothly from the head with intelligent note choices over the V chord (G7), in measures 5 and 6. The ♭7th (F)—and even the 4th (C)—of the V chord (G7) gives a hint of the I chord (C) arriving in measure 7. Measures 7 and 8 show one of his typical improvised composite blues scale resolutions to the I chord.

Performance Tip: Check out the somewhat unusual eight-bar chord progression of I–I–I–I–V–V–I–I.

Section C

One of the hippest characteristics of the blues is when the same riff is repeated over all three chords. The effect can be a dramatic and stunning dynamic highlight in the course of a given song. Walker fashioned a powerful smack to the cortex of the brain when he combined his signature bent diminished voicing with triple stops over the I (C), IV (F7), and V (G7) changes.

Performance Tip: Listen and be aware of how Walker plays in sync with the horn section as the "call," while the piano playing the changes functions as the "response." Meanwhile, the bass walks calmly through the harmonic mayhem as the glue holding it all together!

T-Bone Jumps Again
Section C

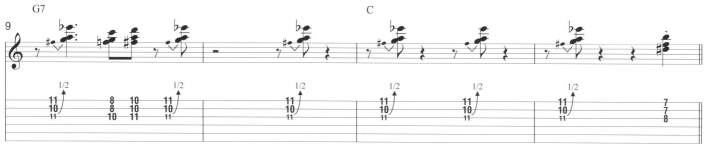

Section E

The one-measure riffs in this section contain many of the same notes as Section C, and are related to the concepts in Section C. The notes function differently depending on which chord the riff is played over. Of distinction is the cool chromatic run on string 3 of Eb–E–F–F#. The result adds lyricism to the blues!

Performance Tip: It is advised to use all four fingers on string 3 for the chromatic line, starting with the index.

T-Bone Jumps Again
Section E

Papa Ain't Salty (1955)
From *T-Bone Blues* (Atlantic)

After his memorable run with Imperial Records, Walker recorded in Chicago for Atlantic Records with some blues cats, including bassist Ransom Knowling. Junior Wells and Jimmy Rogers played on other tracks and recorded the same day. Take note of the stomping Chicago boogie shuffle backing as opposed to the swinging shuffle accompaniment prevalent on his earlier recordings.

Intro

In a pertinent example of what goes around comes around, Walker sounds surprisingly similar to the Westside style of electric blues as propagated by Otis Rush, Buddy Guy, and especially Magic Sam. Like so many others, they were influenced by Walker. Even his tone has that Westside edge and "sting." Furthermore, his vocal delivery and timbre reminds one of Lowell Fulson on his classic "Reconsider, Baby."

Performance Tip: The pickup measure and measures 2 and 6 feature a Walker favorite: a half-step bend of the 4th (C), followed by the 5th (D), root (G), and ♭7th (F) of the I chord (G7). However, his attack is more aggressive than in the past, aided and abetted by his razor-sharp sound. In measure 9, he sounds a bit like Chuck Berry (one of his countless protégés) over the V chord (D7); note how he smacks the G/D (4th/root) followed by a half-step bend of the C (♭7th) on string 3.

Papa Ain't Salty
Intro

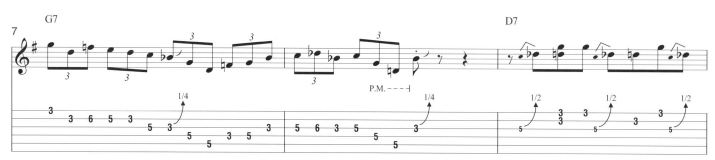

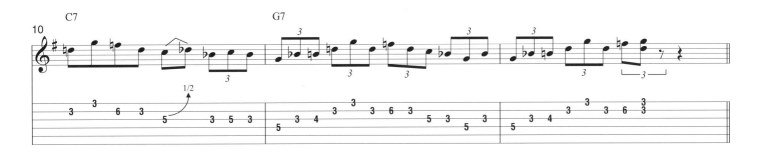

Interlude

Walker swings in with sliding 6/9 chords in what functions as a sumptuously harmonious chord solo. Adding to the effect is a second guitar, likely Jimmy Rogers, providing the "response" in the "call and response" with the same chords in a distinctly midrange, "jazzy" tone.

Performance Tip: Finger the moveable chords, low to high: ring, middle, pinky, and index.

Papa Ain't Salty
Interlude

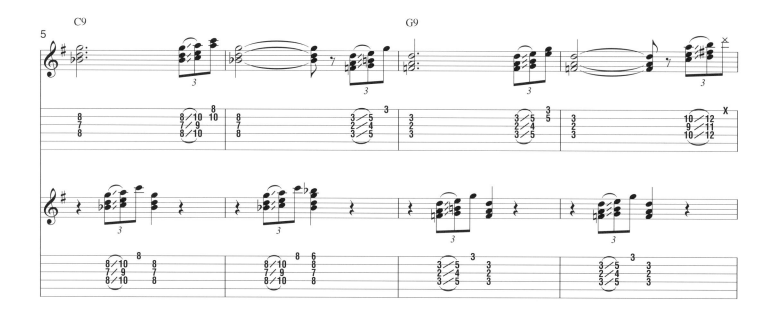

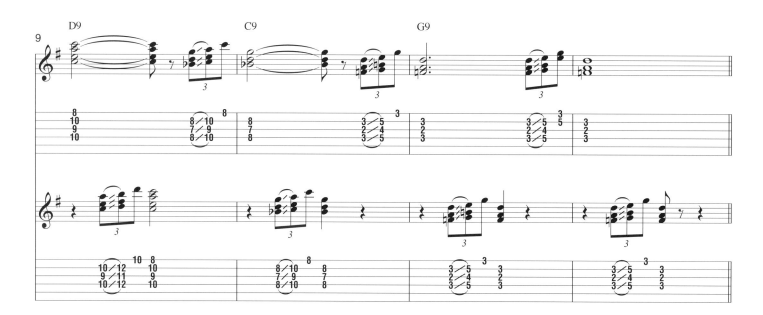

INTEGRAL TECHNIQUES

Photo © Jan Persson/Getty Images

Guitar Manipulation

T-Bone Walker had a highly unusual method of holding his guitar, impacting his picking technique and phrasing.

One significant result was an exceedingly legato style of phrasing with long skeins of notes.

Performance Tip: With few exceptions, Walker played hollow body guitars, their impressive depth and hourglass shape making it fairly easy and comfortable to hold perpendicular against his torso. In addition, as previously mentioned, he appears to have used almost all down strokes across the top of the guitar.

Picking Techniques

Short of imitating the way Walker held his guitar and his penchant for down strokes, it is well worth pursuing a concerted practice regimen to develop accurate, alternate down-up picking in order to emulate his liquid-like flow of notes.

Performance Tip: Joe Pass, the great bluesy-jazz guitarist with likewise impressive legato phrasing, used alternate picking with a caveat: he claimed to always use a pick stroke in the direction of the next string. In other words, if he was moving to a higher string, he used a down stroke. If moving to a lower string, he used an up stroke.

Techniques
Example 1

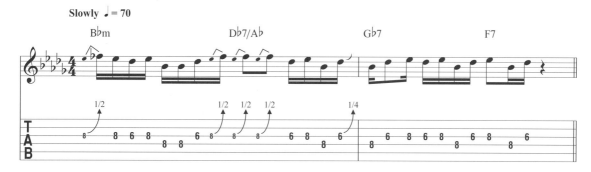

Walker liked to take advantage of the melodic half steps in the composite blues scale by often playing on one string, as seen in this lick.

Performance Tip: Pay attention to the notation indicating even eighth notes in bar 2. While we all strive to make our blues swing, the dynamics of throwing in a measure of even eighths adds "immeasurably" to the art of phrasing.

Techniques Example 2

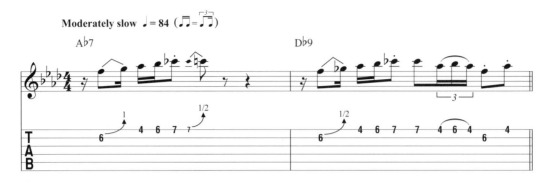

Again, keeping a compact group of composite blues scale notes on one, two, or at most, three strings, compresses the energy level for release in succeeding measures.

Performance Tip: Walker may have utilized all down strokes, but again, alternate picking is highly recommended for these zippy 16th notes.

Techniques Example 3

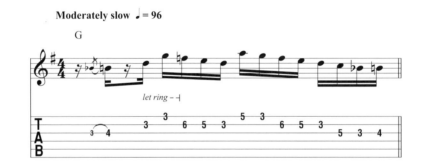

Bending

Aggressive, dramatic over bends were not a cornerstone of the T-Bone Walker guitar style. Instead, he inserted idiomatic quarter-, half-, and whole-step bends with regularity—as natural to him as breathing.

Laying into the "true blue note" a quarter step between the ♭3rd (D♭) and the major 3rd (D) on string 1 in the root position of the B♭ blues scale, Walker rivets attention before releasing it in a run down the scale to the root and ♭3rd (B♭ and D♭).

Performance Tip: Bend with the pinky backed up by the ring, middle, and index fingers.

Techniques Example 4

Though justly lauded for his sophisticated, jazz-inflected style, Walker could whip through repeating figures with blues muscle on occasion.

Performance Tip: As he eschews using a pull-off between the F and the E♭ (as many a contemporary blues guitarist would do), it is suggested to use down-up-down pick strokes. In that manner, the whole-step bends played by the ring finger on string 3 can be achieved using down strokes.

Techniques
Example 5

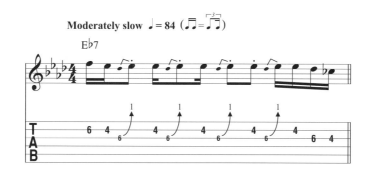

A bend and "slow" release of the same note is an expressive blues guitar technique which has the effect of "slowing" time, brief though that increment may be.

Performance Tip: Bend with the ring finger backed up by the middle and index fingers.

Techniques
Example 6

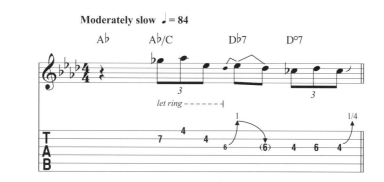

By bending the 9th (E) of the V chord (D7) to the 3rd (F♯) and adding the G/D (4th/root) dyad in this example, Walker nails the tonality.

Performance Tip: Bend with the ring finger backed up by the middle finger while leaving the index in the vicinity of fret 3 to access the G on string 1 and the D on string 2. Observe how it will be necessary to quickly move the ring finger to fret 5 on string 1 for the A note preceding the dyad on beat 4.

Techniques
Example 7

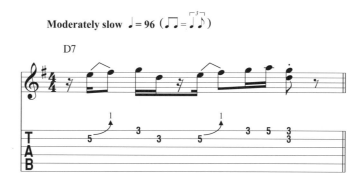

Walker ratchets up the energy quotient with repeating whole-step bends of the D♭ to E♭ on string 3 before releasing it back down to the root of the IV chord (D♭).

Performance Tip: Check out how Walker switches from swung eighths on beats 1 and 2 to even eighths on beats 3 and 4, in what can only be described as a subtle tour-de-force.

Techniques
Example 8

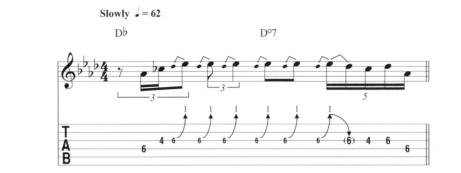

Within the span of one measure, Walker gracefully inserts half- and quarter-step bends, emphasizing the ♭7th (G♭) of the I chord (A♭7), the "true blue note" between the ♭3rd (C♭) and the major 3rd (C), and the ♭7th released to the 6th (F).

Performance Tip: Bend the 6th (F) with the ring finger backed up by the middle and push up the quarter-step bend with the index finger.

Techniques
Example 9

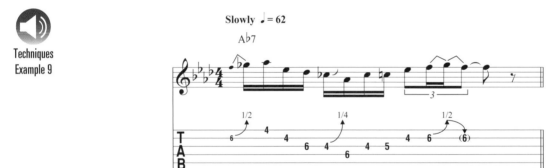

Walker combines the "true blue note" quarter-step bend of the ♭3rd (C♭) on string 1 with the root (A♭) and 5th (E♭) for a slinky, energetic triplet.

Performance Tip: While barring strings 1 and 2 at fret 4, bend the C♭ note at fret 7 with the pinky.

Techniques
Example 10

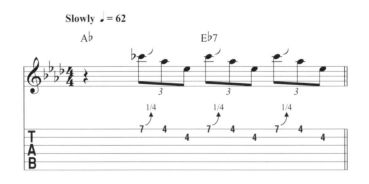

Proving his near infallible intuition, Walker expressively employs a quarter-, half-, and whole-step bend in the span of one measure. Observe how the quarter-step bend to the "true blue note" injects a bit of musical tension against the Ab7, as the half-step bend to Gb does the same for the Eb7#5. However, Walker quickly resolves the tension by following with a whole-step bend to the root (Eb).

Performance Tip: Pull down with the index finger for the quarter-step bend while accessing the other two bends with the ring finger backed up by the middle and index.

Techniques
Example 11

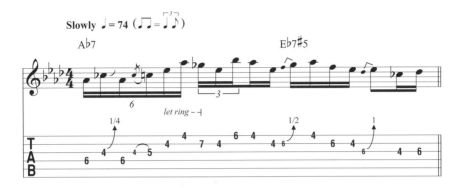

Chord Voicings

T-Bone Walker was not the first blues guitarist to utilize more sophisticated dominant chords like 9ths and 13ths. Oscar Moore, with Nat King Cole, was only one of several to precede him. However, because he was so prominently featured as the star on his records, his accompaniment (as well as his solos) stands out to be "pilfered" by virtually every blues guitarist after him.

Three of Walker's favorite chord voicings appear in these first four measures of a standard 12-bar blues progression as Ab7, Db9/Ab, A9, and Ab9.

Performance Tip: Finger the Ab7 like an open D7 chord. Bend by pushing up as evenly as possible with all three fingers.

Techniques
Example 12

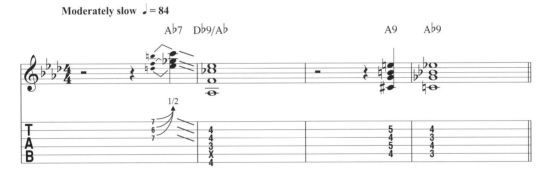

One of Walker's signature rhythm guitar techniques over the third and fourth measures of a standard 12-bar blues form is to begin with a voicing one half step below the tonic chord (Ab9). He then moves up a half step from the tonic chord to the bII chord (A9). Releasing the musical tension on beat 1 of the second measure with the implied tonic chord, he then begins all over again from G9 and eventually reaches his destination of Ab9 on beat 3, saving beat 4 for the bIII chord (C9/G) preceding the IV chord (Db9) in the following measure (not shown).

Techniques
Example 13

STYLISTIC DNA

What should be apparent by this point in the study of T-Bone Walker is his propensity to often play in flat keys. While virtually all singers need to find keys suited to their range, in his case it is more likely due to his consistent arrangements with horn sections, which are more naturally comfortable in keys such as Bb and Ab.

Intros

This brilliant four-measure Intro is a master class on how to arrange chords and fills into a complete, stand-alone musical statement. Even the subtle bass accompaniment is superfluous. Notice how the Intro contains two similar two-measure sections which advance harmonically through the i chord (Bbm), bIII chord (Db7/Ab), bVI power chord (Gb5), and V chord (F7). Broken chord fragments and bass lines connect the changes seamlessly. At the end of beat 2 in measure 1, the use of sliding minor 3rds connecting Bbm to Db7/Ab stands out as an unusually creative choice, even for Walker.

Performance Tip: Play the sliding 3rds with the middle and ring fingers, low to high. In this manner, it will be simply a matter of placing the index finger at fret 3 on string 4 to access the broken Db7/Ab chord on beat 4.

DNA
Example 1

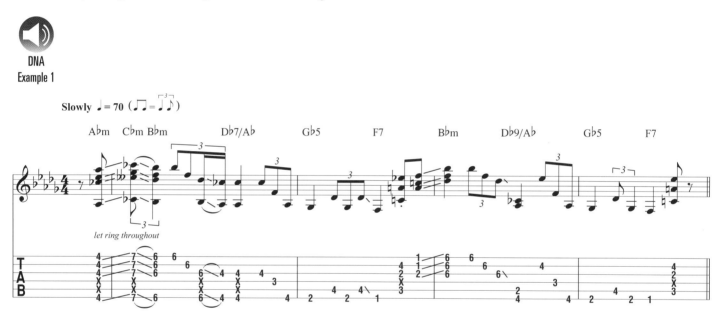

Moving from V–#V–V has been, and continues to be, a simple yet effective way to commence a blues tune—and Walker used it often. Like so many elements of the blues, it creates tension followed by release. Note how the Ab composite blues scale lick on beat 4 of measure 2 *could* be seen as indicating the I chord (Ab) in the following measure (not shown).

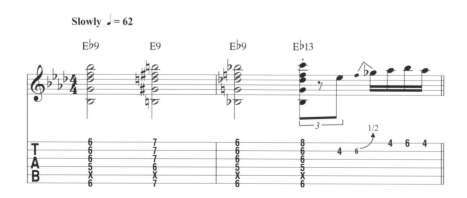

DNA
Example 2

Walker combines broken chords, 13th-note chord extensions, and a short lick from the Ab composite blues scale in a virtuosic display worthy of two guitarists. The two measures of harmony accede to dramatic musical gravity via chord changes that are essentially a typical I–V progression: Ab13/C (I)–Gb13 (bVII)–Fb13 (bVI)–Eb7 (V).

Performance Tip: The root notes of the four chords, if present, would all be on string 5 and played with the middle finger as if they were standard 9th chords. Hence, if the hand is positioned in that way, it will make for easy access to the 13th and 9th notes on string 1. Observe how Walker indicates Eb7 with the most minimal means: Db/G fretted with the index and middle fingers, low to high. In this manner, his hand is in an advantageous position to grab the following lick with the index and ring fingers.

DNA
Example 3

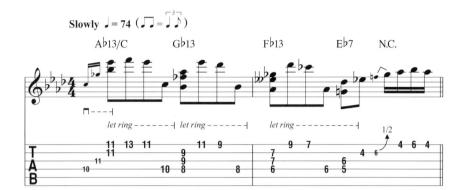

Turnarounds

Walker takes a basic I–IV–I–V turnaround and "turns" it into a hip progression of:

I: A♭–A♭7

IV: D♭7–D°7

I: A♭7/E♭

V: E♭7

Performance Tip: Notice the A9 chord on beat 4 of the second measure, inserted as a "grace chord" leading to the A♭9 resolution in the next bar (not shown).

DNA
Example 4

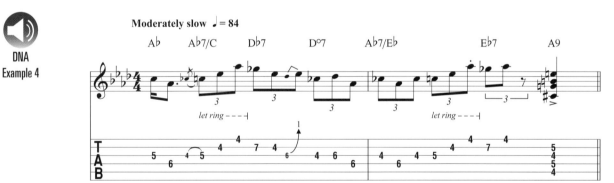

With the turnaround changes simplified to I (G) and V (D7), Walker employs some of his standard single-note lines kicking off both measures—including his signature 3rd (B), 5th (D), and root (G) lick. However, being cognizant of the change to the V chord on beats 3 and 4 of the next measure, he makes sure to highlight the root (D) of D7 along with the 5th (A), ending on the 4th (G) to encourage forward momentum into the I chord (G) in the following measure (not shown).

DNA
Example 5

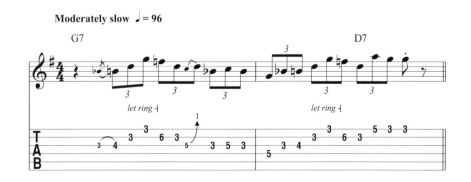

As the turnaround features typical I (G), IV (C/D), and V (D7) chords, Walker naturally navigates the changes with precision and subtlety. Over the I chord in the first measure, he drops in his 3rd (B), 5th (D), and root (G) "calling card," while over the IV chord he intelligently sustains the 3rd (E), followed shortly thereafter by the root (C). In the final measure, he takes a longer route up the root position of the G composite blues scale over the I chord and then sustains the root of the V chord (D).

Performance Tip: Like Example 5, Walker plays a G triad on beat 4 of the last measure as anticipation of the I chord (G7) in the following measure (not shown).

DNA
Example 6

Closing out the first Verse, Walker "rips" 16th and 32nd notes in a tour-de-force of dynamic bending and undulating runs. In addition, his command of the composite blues scale is a virtual blues guitar workshop.

Performance Tip: Of the numerous invaluable lessons to be learned from studying the essential style of T-Bone Walker, one of the most critical is to know when to halt an onslaught of eighth or 16th notes with another technique, such as a bend, or even a musical rest. Another approach is to "take in a breath" before a long run of notes and then let it out normally while chipping away at a scale. When finished "exhaling," stop the run and repeat the cycle as desired.

DNA
Example 7

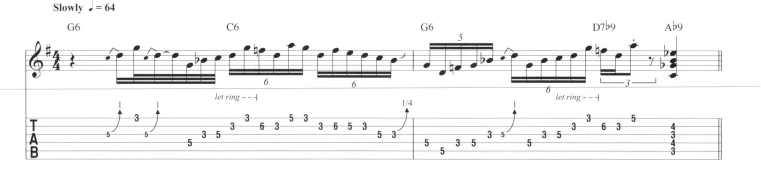

MUST HEAR

Though the period 1942–1954 is rightfully considered his classic era, T-Bone Walker never made a bad record—even when he attempted more contemporary material in the '60s. Be aware that many duplicate recordings have been issued and are still in print.

The Complete Recordings of T-Bone Walker 1940–1954 (1990)

This six-disk box set on Mosaic Records is long out of print, but well worth the search. It is considered to be the "Rosetta Stone" of post-war electric blues recordings.

Essential Tracks

I Got a Break Baby
Mean Old World
You Don't Love Me Blues
T-Bone Boogie
It's a Low Down Dirty Deal
I Know Your Wig Is Gone
T-Bone Jumps Again
Call It Stormy Monday
Hypin' Woman Blues
The Natural Blues
Description Blues
T-Bone Shuffle
Plain Old Down Home Blues
Glamour Girl
Strollin' with Bone
The Hustle Is On
Tell Me What's the Reason
Cold, Cold Feeling
I Got the Blues
Party Girl
Railroad Station Blues
Vida Lee

T-Bone Walker: The Ultimate Collection 1929–57 (2014)

This five-disk set contains many duplicates from the Mosaic box set along with other classics.

Essential Tracks

Sail On Boogie
T-Bone Blues
Evening
Hard Pain Blues
Lonesome Woman Blues
I Want a Little Girl
I'm Still in Love with You
West Side Baby
No Reason
Alimony Blues
I Get So Weary
Get These Blues off Me
Street Walkin' Woman
Love Is Just a Gamble
High Society

Every Day I Have the Blues (2014)

Walker presents the blues in a more contemporary—even funky—style, from 1969.

Essential Tracks

Sail On
For B.B. King
Stormy Monday Blues (Live at Carnegie Hall, 1970)
Sail On (Live at Carnegie Hall, 1970)

Funky Town (2017)

Arguably the best of his later recordings, from 1969.

Essential Tracks

Goin' to Funky Town
Going to Build Me a Playhouse
I Wish My Baby (Would Come Home at Night)

MUST SEE

Unfortunately, precious little quality video footage exists for many of the greatest post-war blues guitarists. Fortunately, this is not the case for T-Bone Walker. Nothing exists from the '40s, but check out these exciting, instructional titles from the '50s and '60s.

On DVD

T-Bone Walker Guitar Signature Licks (Hal Leonard), 2002
Instructional DVD performed by Duke Robillard, with rhythm guitar and bass tracks provided by author.

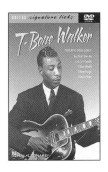

On YouTube

T-Bone Walker – Live 1962–1967
Excellent set including selections from the BBC in London, in 1965.

T-Bone Walker "Hey Baby," 1965
Hard-swinging performance from the BBC featuring his propulsive accompaniment.

T-Bone Walker w/Jazz at the Philharmonic Live in UK 1966
"Bone" is not intimidated by the jazz cats Dizzy Gillespie, Clark Terry, James Moody, Zoot Sims, and Teddy Wilson, as he "tutors" them on the "down home" blues.

T-Bone Walker – Don't Throw Your Love on Me So Strong
Just the one track, but a magnificent performance.

T-Bone Walker and B.B. King – Sweet Sixteen
The "father" and the "son" in an historic performance at the 1967 Monterey Pop Festival.

T-Bone Walker – Call It Stormy Monday
Low-resolution video, but great audio on a definitive version of his immortal classic.

T-Bone Walker & Shakey Jake Harris – "Call If You Need Me"
Rare and unusual duo performance featuring Walker playing a low-volume country blues in the key of E behind the vocals of Harris.

GUITAR NOTATION LEGEND

Guitar music can be notated three different ways: on a *musical staff*, in *tablature*, and in *rhythm slashes*.

RHYTHM SLASHES are written above the staff. Strum chords in the rhythm indicated. Use the chord diagrams found at the top of the first page of the transcription for the appropriate chord voicings. Round noteheads indicate single notes.

THE MUSICAL STAFF shows pitches and rhythms and is divided by bar lines into measures. Pitches are named after the first seven letters of the alphabet.

TABLATURE graphically represents the guitar fingerboard. Each horizontal line represents a string, and each number represents a fret.

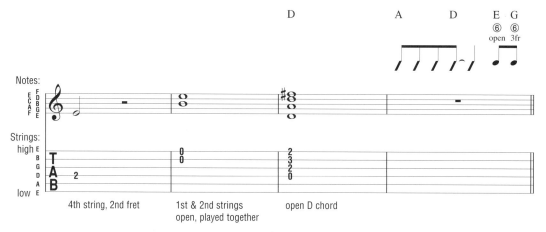

4th string, 2nd fret

1st & 2nd strings open, played together

open D chord

Definitions for Special Guitar Notation

HALF-STEP BEND: Strike the note and bend up 1/2 step.

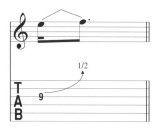

WHOLE-STEP BEND: Strike the note and bend up one step.

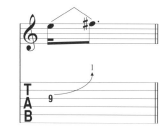

GRACE NOTE BEND: Strike the note and immediately bend up as indicated.

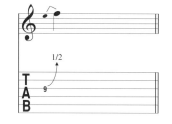

SLIGHT (MICROTONE) BEND: Strike the note and bend up 1/4 step.

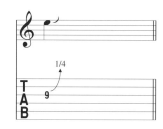

BEND AND RELEASE: Strike the note and bend up as indicated, then release back to the original note. Only the first note is struck.

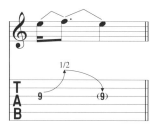

PRE-BEND: Bend the note as indicated, then strike it.

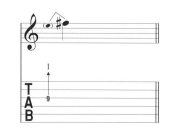

PRE-BEND AND RELEASE: Bend the note as indicated. Strike it and release the bend back to the original note.

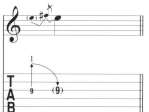

UNISON BEND: Strike the two notes simultaneously and bend the lower note up to the pitch of the higher.

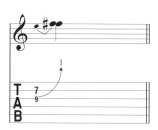

VIBRATO: The string is vibrated by rapidly bending and releasing the note with the fretting hand.

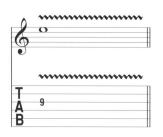

WIDE VIBRATO: The pitch is varied to a greater degree by vibrating with the fretting hand.

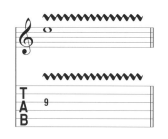

HAMMER-ON: Strike the first (lower) note with one finger, then sound the higher note (on the same string) with another finger by fretting it without picking.

PULL-OFF: Place both fingers on the notes to be sounded. Strike the first note and without picking, pull the finger off to sound the second (lower) note.

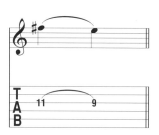

LEGATO SLIDE: Strike the first note and then slide the same fret-hand finger up or down to the second note. The second note is not struck.

SHIFT SLIDE: Same as legato slide, except the second note is struck.

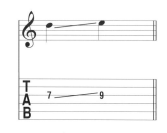

TRILL: Very rapidly alternate between the notes indicated by continuously hammering on and pulling off.

TAPPING: Hammer ("tap") the fret indicated with the pick-hand index or middle finger and pull off to the note fretted by the fret hand.

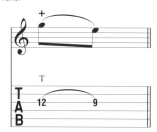

NATURAL HARMONIC: Strike the note while the fret-hand lightly touches the string directly over the fret indicated.

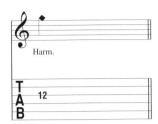

Harm.

PINCH HARMONIC: The note is fretted normally and a harmonic is produced by adding the edge of the thumb or the tip of the index finger of the pick hand to the normal pick attack.

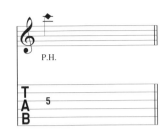

P.H.

HARP HARMONIC: The note is fretted normally and a harmonic is produced by gently resting the pick hand's index finger directly above the indicated fret (in parentheses) while the pick hand's thumb or pick assists by plucking the appropriate string.

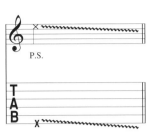

H.H.

PICK SCRAPE: The edge of the pick is rubbed down (or up) the string, producing a scratchy sound.

P.S.

MUFFLED STRINGS: A percussive sound is produced by laying the fret hand across the string(s) without depressing, and striking them with the pick hand.

PALM MUTING: The note is partially muted by the pick hand lightly touching the string(s) just before the bridge.

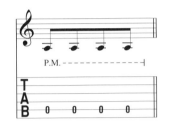

P.M. - - - - - - - - - - -

RAKE: Drag the pick across the strings indicated with a single motion.

rake - - -

TREMOLO PICKING: The note is picked as rapidly and continuously as possible.

ARPEGGIATE: Play the notes of the chord indicated by quickly rolling them from bottom to top.

VIBRATO BAR DIVE AND RETURN: The pitch of the note or chord is dropped a specified number of steps (in rhythm), then returned to the original pitch.

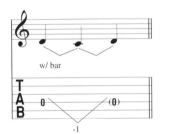

w/ bar

VIBRATO BAR SCOOP: Depress the bar just before striking the note, then quickly release the bar.

w/ bar - - - - - - - - - -

VIBRATO BAR DIP: Strike the note and then immediately drop a specified number of steps, then release back to the original pitch.

w/ bar - - - - - - - - - - -

Additional Musical Definitions

> (accent)	• Accentuate note (play it louder).	
^ (accent)	• Accentuate note with great intensity.	
• (staccato)	• Play the note short.	
⊓	• Downstroke	
V	• Upstroke	
D.S. al Coda	• Go back to the sign (𝄋), then play until the measure marked "*To Coda*," then skip to the section labelled "**Coda**."	
D.C. al Fine	• Go back to the beginning of the song and play until the measure marked "*Fine*" (end).	

Rhy. Fig. • Label used to recall a recurring accompaniment pattern (usually chordal).

Riff • Label used to recall composed, melodic lines (usually single notes) which recur.

Fill • Label used to identify a brief melodic figure which is to be inserted into the arrangement.

Rhy. Fill • A chordal version of a Fill.

tacet • Instrument is silent (drops out).

• Repeat measures between signs.

1. 2.

• When a repeated section has different endings, play the first ending only the first time and the second ending only the second time.

NOTE: Tablature numbers in parentheses mean:
  1. The note is being sustained over a system (note in standard notation is tied), or
  2. The note is sustained, but a new articulation (such as a hammer-on, pull-off, slide or vibrato) begins, or
  3. The note is a barely audible "ghost" note (note in standard notation is also in parentheses).

MASTER THE *Blues*

With guitar instruction from Hal Leonard
All books include notes and tab.

Hal Leonard Guitar Method – Blues Guitar
by Greg Koch
The complete guide to learning blues guitar uses real blues songs to teach you the basics of rhythm and lead blues guitar in the style of B.B. King, Buddy Guy, Eric Clapton, and many others. Lessons include: 12-bar blues; chords, scales and licks; vibrato and string bending; riffs, turnarounds, and boogie patterns; and more!
00697326 Book/CD Pack $16.99

Blues Deluxe
by Dave Rubin
Not only does this deluxe edition provide accurate transcriptions of ten blues classics plus performance notes and artist bios, it also includes a CD with the *original Alligator Records recordings* of every song! Tunes: Are You Losing Your Mind? (Buddy Guy) • Don't Take Advantage of Me (Johnny Winter) • Gravel Road (Magic Slim) • Somebody Loan Me a Dime (Fenton Robinson) • and more.
00699918 Book/CD Pack.....................$24.99

Art of the Shuffle
by Dave Rubin
This method book explores shuffle, boogie and swing rhythms for guitar. Includes tab and notation, and covers Delta, country, Chicago, Kansas City, Texas, New Orleans, West Coast, and bebop blues. Also includes audio for demonstration of each style and to jam along with.
00695005 Book/CD Pack....................$19.95

Power Trio Blues
by Dave Rubin
This book/CD pack details how to play electric guitar in a trio with bass and drums. Boogie, shuffle, and slow blues rhythms, licks, double stops, chords, and bass patterns are presented for full and exciting blues. A CD with the music examples performed by a smokin' power trio is included for play-along instruction and jamming.
00695028 Book/CD Pack....................$19.99

100 Blues Lessons
Guitar Lesson Goldmine
by John Heussenstamm and Chad Johnson
A huge variety of blues guitar styles and techniques are covered, including: turnarounds, hammer-ons and pull-offs, slides, the blues scale, 12-bar blues, double stops, muting techniques, hybrid picking, fingerstyle blues, and much more!
00696452 Book/2-CD Pack.................$24.99

Electric Slide Guitar
by David Hamburger
This book/audio method explores the basic fundamentals of slide guitar: from selecting a slide and proper setup of the guitar, to open and standard tuning. Plenty of music examples are presented showing sample licks as well as backup/rhythm slide work. Each section also examines techniques and solos in the style of the best slide guitarists, including Duane Allman, Dave Hole, Ry Cooder, Bonnie Raitt, Muddy Waters, Johnny Winter and Elmore James.
00695022 Book/CD Pack....................$19.95

101 Must-Know Blues Licks
A Quick, Easy Reference for All Guitarists
by Wolf Marshall
Now you can add authentic blues feel and flavor to your playing! Here are 101 definitive licks – plus a demonstration CD – from every major blues guitar style, neatly organized into easy-to-use categories. They're all here, including Delta blues, jump blues, country blues, Memphis blues, Texas blues, West Coast blues, Chicago blues, and British blues.
00695318 Book/CD Pack....................$17.95

Fretboard Roadmaps Blues Guitar
for Acoustic and Electric Guitar
by Fred Sokolow
These essential fretboard patterns are roadmaps that all great blues guitarists know and use. This book teaches how to: play lead and rhythm anywhere on the fretboard, in any key; play a variety of lead guitar styles; play chords and progressions anywhere on the fretboard, in any key; expand chord vocabulary; learn to think musicially, the way the pros do.
00695350 Book/CD Pack....................$14.95

The Road to Robert Johnson
The Genesis and Evolution of Blues in the Delta from the Late 1800s Through 1938
by Edward Komara
This book traces the development of the legendary Robert Johnson's music in light of the people and songs that directly and indirectly influenced him. It includes much information about life in the Delta from the late 1800s to Johnson's controversial death in 1938, and features fascinating historical photos, maps, musical examples, and much more.
00695388..$14.95

12-Bar Blues
by Dave Rubin
The term "12-bar blues" has become synonymous with blues music and is the basis for an incredible body of jazz, rock 'n' roll, and other forms of popular music. This book/CD pack is solely devoted to providing guitarists with all the technical tools necessary for playing 12-bar blues with authority. The CD includes 24 full-band tracks. Covers: boogie, shuffle, swing, riff, and jazzy blues progressions; Chicago, minor, slow, bebop, and other blues styles; soloing, intros, turnarounds, and more.
00695187 Book/CD Pack.....................$18.99

Smokin' Blues Guitar
by Smokin' Joe Kubek with Dave Rubin
Texas blues guitar legend Smokin' Joe Kubek and acclaimed author and music historian Dave Rubin have teamed up to create this one-of-a-kind DVD/book bundle, featuring a high-definition DVD with Smokin' Joe himself demonstrating loads of electric blues licks, riffs, concepts, and techniques straight from his extensive arsenal. The companion book, co-written with Dave Rubin, provides standard notation and tablature for every smokin' example on the DVD, as well as bonus instructional material, and much more!
00696469 Book/DVD Pack.................$24.99

Blues You Can Use Chord Book
by John Ganapes
A reference guide to blues, R&B, jazz, and rock rhythm guitar, with hundreds of voicings, chord theory construction, chord progressions and exercises and much more. The Blues You Can Use Book Of Guitar Chords is useful for the beginner to advanced player.
00695082..$14.95

More Blues You Can Use
by John Ganapes
A complete guide to learning blues guitar, covering scales, rhythms, chords, patterns, rakes, techniques, and more. CD includes 13 full-demo solos.
00695165 Book/CD Pack....................$19.95

Blues Licks You Can Use
by John Ganapes
Contains music and performance notes for 75 hot lead phrases, covering styles including up-tempo and slow blues, jazz-blues, shuffle blues, swing blues and more! CD features full-band examples.
00695386 Book/CD Pack....................$16.95

HAL•LEONARD®
CORPORATION
7777 W. BLUEMOUND RD. P.O. BOX 13819 MILWAUKEE, WI 53213

www.halleonard.com
Prices, availability, and contents subject to change without notice. Some products may not be available outside the U.S.A.

Get Better at Guitar

...with these Great Guitar Instruction Books from Hal Leonard!

101 GUITAR TIPS
INCLUDES TAB

STUFF ALL THE PROS KNOW AND USE
by Adam St. James
This book contains invaluable guidance on everything from scales and music theory to truss rod adjustments, proper recording studio set-ups, and much more. The book also features snippets of advice from some of the most celebrated guitarists and producers in the music business, including B.B. King, Steve Vai, Joe Satriani, Warren Haynes, Laurence Juber, Pete Anderson, Tom Dowd and others, culled from the author's hundreds of interviews.
00695737 Book/Online Audio $16.99

AMAZING PHRASING
INCLUDES TAB

50 WAYS TO IMPROVE YOUR IMPROVISATIONAL SKILLS
by Tom Kolb
This book/audio pack explores all the main components necessary for crafting well-balanced rhythmic and melodic phrases. It also explains how these phrases are put together to form cohesive solos. Many styles are covered – rock, blues, jazz, fusion, country, Latin, funk and more – and all of the concepts are backed up with musical examples. The companion audio contains 89 demos for listening, and most tracks feature full-band backing.
00695583 Book/Online Audio $19.99

BLUES YOU CAN USE – 2ND EDITION
by John Ganapes
This comprehensive source for learning blues guitar is designed to develop both your lead and rhythm playing. Includes: 21 complete solos • blues chords, progressions and riffs • turnarounds • movable scales and soloing techniques • string bending • utilizing the entire fingerboard • and more. This second edition now includes audio and video access online!
00142420 Book/Online Media................................$19.99

FRETBOARD MASTERY
INCLUDES TAB

by Troy Stetina
Untangle the mysterious regions of the guitar fretboard and unlock your potential. *Fretboard Mastery* familiarizes you with all the shapes you need to know by applying them in real musical examples, thereby reinforcing and reaffirming your newfound knowledge. The result is a much higher level of comprehension and retention.
00695331 Book/Online Audio $19.99

FRETBOARD ROADMAPS – 2ND EDITION

ESSENTIAL GUITAR PATTERNS THAT ALL THE PROS KNOW AND USE
by Fred Sokolow
The updated edition of this bestseller features more songs, updated lessons, audio tracks! Learn to play lead and rhythm anywhere on the fretboard, in any key; play a variety of lead guitar styles; play chords and progressions anywhere on the fretboard; expand your chord vocabulary; and learn to think musically – the way the pros do.
00695941 Book/Online Audio $15.99

GUITAR AEROBICS
INCLUDES TAB

A 52-WEEK, ONE-LICK-PER-DAY WORKOUT PROGRAM FOR DEVELOPING, IMPROVING & MAINTAINING GUITAR TECHNIQUE
by Troy Nelson
From the former editor of *Guitar One* magazine, here is a daily dose of vitamins to keep your chops fine tuned! Musical styles include rock, blues, jazz, metal, country, and funk. Techniques taught include alternate picking, arpeggios, sweep picking, string skipping, legato, string bending, and rhythm guitar. These exercises will increase speed, and improve dexterity and pick- and fret-hand accuracy. The accompanying audio includes all 365 workout licks plus play-along grooves in every style at eight different metronome settings.
00695946 Book/Online Audio $19.99

GUITAR CLUES
INCLUDES TAB

OPERATION PENTATONIC
by Greg Koch
Join renowned guitar master Greg Koch as he clues you in to a wide variety of fun and valuable pentatonic scale applications. Whether you're new to improvising or have been doing it for a while, this book/audio pack will provide loads of delicious licks and tricks that you can use right away, from volume swells and chicken pickin' to intervallic and chordal ideas. The online audio includes 65 demo and play-along tracks.
00695827 Book/Online Audio $19.99

INTRODUCTION TO GUITAR TONE & EFFECTS
by David M. Brewster
This book/audio pack teaches the basics of guitar tones and effects, with online audio examples. Readers will learn about: overdrive, distortion and fuzz • using equalizers • modulation effects • reverb and delay • multi-effect processors • and more.
00695766 Book/Online Audio $16.99

PICTURE CHORD ENCYCLOPEDIA

This comprehensive guitar chord resource for all playing styles and levels features five voicings of 44 chord qualities for all twelve keys – 2,640 chords in all! For each, there is a clearly illustrated chord frame, as well as *an actual photo* of the chord being played! Includes info on basic fingering principles, open chords and barre chords, partial chords and broken-set forms, and more.
00695224..$19.95

SCALE CHORD RELATIONSHIPS
INCLUDES TAB

by Michael Mueller & Jeff Schroedl
This book teaches players how to determine which scales to play with which chords, so guitarists will never have to fear chord changes again! This book/audio pack explains how to: recognize keys • analyze chord progressions • use the modes • play over nondiatonic harmony • use harmonic and melodic minor scales • use symmetrical scales such as chromatic, whole-tone and diminished scales • incorporate exotic scales such as Hungarian major and Gypsy minor • and much more!
00695563 Book/Online Audio $14.99

SPEED MECHANICS FOR LEAD GUITAR
INCLUDES TAB

Take your playing to the stratosphere with the most advanced lead book by this proven heavy metal author. *Speed Mechanics* is the ultimate technique book for developing the kind of speed and precision in today's explosive playing styles. Learn the fastest ways to achieve speed and control, secrets to make your practice time really count, and how to open your ears and make your musical ideas more solid and tangible. Packed with over 200 vicious exercises including Troy's scorching version of "Flight of the Bumblebee." Music and examples demonstrated on the accompanying online audio.
00699323 Book/Online Audio $19.99

TOTAL ROCK GUITAR
INCLUDES TAB

A COMPLETE GUIDE TO LEARNING ROCK GUITAR
by Troy Stetina
This unique and comprehensive source for learning rock guitar is designed to develop both lead and rhythm playing. It covers: getting a tone that rocks • open chords, power chords and barre chords • riffs, scales and licks • string bending, strumming, palm muting, harmonics and alternate picking • all rock styles • and much more. The examples are in standard notation with chord grids and tab, and the audio includes full-band backing for all 22 songs.
00695246 Book/Online Audio $19.99

Visit Hal Leonard Online at
www.halleonard.com

HAL•LEONARD®

Prices, contents, and availability subject to change without notice.

GUITAR *signature licks*

Signature Licks book/audio packs provide a step-by-step breakdown of "right from the record" riffs, licks, and solos so you can jam along with your favorite bands. They contain performance notes and an overview of each artist's or group's style, with note-for-note transcriptions in notes and tab. The CDs or online audio tracks feature full-band demos at both normal and slow speeds.

AC/DC
14041352.....................$22.99

AEROSMITH 1973-1979
00695106.....................$22.95

AEROSMITH 1979-1998
00695219.....................$22.95

DUANE ALLMAN
00696042.....................$22.99

BEST OF CHET ATKINS
00695752.....................$24.99

AVENGED SEVENFOLD
00696473.....................$22.99

BEST OF THE BEATLES FOR ACOUSTIC GUITAR
00695453.....................$22.99

THE BEATLES BASS
00695283.....................$22.99

THE BEATLES HITS
00695049.....................$24.95

JEFF BECK
00696427.....................$22.99

BEST OF GEORGE BENSON
00695418.....................$22.99

BEST OF BLACK SABBATH
00695249.....................$22.95

BLUES BREAKERS WITH JOHN MAYALL & ERIC CLAPTON
00696374.....................$22.99

BON JOVI
00696380.....................$22.99

ROY BUCHANAN
00696654.....................$22.99

KENNY BURRELL
00695830.....................$24.99

BEST OF CHARLIE CHRISTIAN
00695584.....................$24.99

BEST OF ERIC CLAPTON
00695038.....................$24.99

ERIC CLAPTON – FROM THE ALBUM UNPLUGGED
00695250.....................$24.95

BEST OF CREAM
00695251.....................$22.95

CREEDANCE CLEARWATER REVIVAL
00695924.....................$22.95

DEEP PURPLE – GREATEST HITS
00695625.....................$22.99

DREAM THEATER
00111943.....................$24.99

TOMMY EMMANUEL
00696409.....................$22.99

ESSENTIAL JAZZ GUITAR
00695875.....................$19.99

FAMOUS ROCK GUITAR SOLOS
00695590.....................$19.95

FLEETWOOD MAC
00696416.....................$22.99

BEST OF FOO FIGHTERS
00695481.....................$24.95

ROBBEN FORD
00695903.....................$22.95

BEST OF GRANT GREEN
00695747.....................$22.99

PETER GREEN
00145386.....................$22.99

THE GUITARS OF ELVIS – 2ND ED.
00174800.....................$22.99

BEST OF GUNS N' ROSES
00695183.....................$24.99

THE BEST OF BUDDY GUY
00695186.....................$22.99

JIM HALL
00695848.....................$24.99

JIMI HENDRIX
00696560.....................$24.99

JIMI HENDRIX – VOLUME 2
00695835.....................$24.99

JOHN LEE HOOKER
00695894.....................$22.99

BEST OF JAZZ GUITAR
00695586.....................$24.99

ERIC JOHNSON
00699317.....................$24.99

ROBERT JOHNSON
00695264.....................$22.95

BARNEY KESSEL
00696009.....................$24.99

THE ESSENTIAL ALBERT KING
00695713.....................$22.95

B.B. KING – BLUES LEGEND
00696039.....................$22.99

B.B. KING – THE DEFINITIVE COLLECTION
00695635.....................$22.95

B.B. KING – MASTER BLUESMAN
00699923.....................$24.99

MARK KNOPFLER
00695178.....................$24.99

LYNYRD SKYNYRD
00695872.....................$24.99

THE BEST OF YNGWIE MALMSTEEN
00695669.....................$24.99

BEST OF PAT MARTINO
00695632.....................$24.99

MEGADETH
00696421.....................$22.99

WES MONTGOMERY
00695387.....................$24.99

BEST OF NIRVANA
00695483.....................$24.95

VERY BEST OF OZZY OSBOURNE
00695431.....................$22.99

BRAD PAISLEY
00696379.....................$22.99

BEST OF JOE PASS
00695730.....................$22.99

JACO PASTORIUS
00695544.....................$24.95

TOM PETTY
00696021.....................$22.99

PINK FLOYD
00103659.....................$24.99

BEST OF QUEEN
00695097.....................$24.99

RADIOHEAD
00109304.....................$24.99

BEST OF RAGE AGAINST THE MACHINE
00695480.....................$24.95

RED HOT CHILI PEPPERS
00695173.....................$22.95

RED HOT CHILI PEPPERS – GREATEST HITS
00695828.....................$24.99

JERRY REED
00118236.....................$22.99

BEST OF DJANGO REINHARDT
00695660.....................$24.99

BEST OF ROCK 'N' ROLL GUITAR
00695559.....................$22.99

BEST OF ROCKABILLY GUITAR
00695785.....................$19.99

BEST OF CARLOS SANTANA
00174664.....................$22.99

BEST OF JOE SATRIANI
00695216.....................$22.95

SLASH
00696576.....................$22.99

SLAYER
00121281.....................$22.99

THE BEST OF SOUL GUITAR
00695703.....................$19.95

BEST OF SOUTHERN ROCK
00695560.....................$19.95

STEELY DAN
00696015.....................$22.99

MIKE STERN
00695800.....................$24.99

BEST OF SURF GUITAR
00695822.....................$19.99

STEVE VAI
00673247.....................$24.99

STEVE VAI – ALIEN LOVE SECRETS: THE NAKED VAMPS
00695223.....................$22.95

STEVE VAI – FIRE GARDEN: THE NAKED VAMPS
00695166.....................$22.95

STEVE VAI – THE ULTRA ZONE: NAKED VAMPS
00695684.....................$22.95

VAN HALEN
00110227.....................$24.99

STEVIE RAY VAUGHAN – 2ND ED.
00699316.....................$24.95

THE GUITAR STYLE OF STEVIE RAY VAUGHAN
00695155.....................$24.95

BEST OF THE VENTURES
00695772.....................$19.95

THE WHO – 2ND ED.
00695561.....................$22.95

JOHNNY WINTER
00695951.....................$22.99

YES
00113120.....................$22.99

NEIL YOUNG – GREATEST HITS
00695988.....................$22.99

BEST OF ZZ TOP
00695738.....................$24.99

HAL•LEONARD®
www.halleonard.com

COMPLETE DESCRIPTIONS AND SONGLISTS ONLINE!
Prices, contents and availability subject to change without notice.

0719
305